I0813620

GARDEN EXOTICA

International Plant-Based Fusion Cuisine

Photography by

BABITA SHRESTHA & CHARLES F MORELAND III

Cooked, Written, and Designed by

BABITA SHRESTHA

This book is a publication of

Red Lightning Books
1320 East 10th Street
Bloomington, Indiana 47405 USA

redlightningbooks.com

For customers in the European Union with safety or GPSR concerns, please contact Mare Nostrum Group B.V., Mauritskade 21D, 1091 GC Amsterdam, The Netherlands. Email: gpsr@mare-nostrum.co.uk.

ISBN 978-1-68435-233-3 (hdbk.)
ISBN 978-1-68435-235-7 (ebook)
ISBN 978-1-68435-234-0 (web PDF)

First printing 2025

To my dear daughter Saraswati and amazing husband Charles,
Thank you for bringing joy to my life every day.

CONTENTS

Introduction

A Culinary Journey Rooted in Tradition and Growth

Life is a beautiful symphony of seasons, from the vital burst of spring life to the abundant harvest of autumn. In Nepal, where I come from, generations have cultivated a deep connection to the land, passing down the art of home cooking and cultivating their own food. My childhood memories are filled with the warmth of the kitchen, the laughter of loved ones, and the intoxicating fragrance of fresh ingredients dancing in the air. Surrounded by these traditions, I learned the joy of creation and the profound nourishment of home-cooked meals—a legacy I now share with my daughter.

My passion for growing food blossomed at a young age, following in the footsteps of my grandfather. He taught me the language of the soil, the patience required for nurturing life, and the magic of harvesting the bounty of the earth. This love for homegrown ingredients has become an essential thread woven into the fabric of my everyday cooking, a tradition I cherish and continue here in the United States with my family. Now, witnessing my daughter embrace the same love for healthy, home-cooked meals brings me immense joy. It's a testament to the enduring power of cultural heritage, passed down not only through stories but also through the simple act of cooking together.

Garden Exotica is a celebration of this love for plant-based cooking, featuring sixty-one flavorful and nutritious recipes inspired by the vast array of global cuisines. Whether you're a seasoned gardener with a flourishing backyard oasis or a busy city dweller reliant on local markets, this book offers a welcoming space to explore the world of vegetarian and vegan dishes. Forget about overly complicated techniques or elusive ingredients—here, you'll find accessible and adaptable recipes that are perfect for incorporating into your daily routine.

This book is not just a collection of recipes; it's an invitation to embark on a culinary journey. The book is divided into five distinct sections, each designed to empower you as you navigate the kitchen with confidence. We'll begin by demystifying the art of homemade sauces, versatile building blocks that can add layers of exotic flavor to any dish. Next, enjoy the ride from appetizer to entrée with our collection of salads, soups, breads, and savory main courses. My personal interpretations of dishes from various cultures are not strict replications of tradition; rather, they are a fusion of global influences and my own culinary perspective, adapted for the everyday home cook.

My goal is to inspire you to create healthy and exquisite plant-based meals from scratch, using simple and readily available ingredients. With each dish, I want to enliven your adventurous spirit, encouraging you to experiment and embrace new flavors.

Throughout the cookbook, you'll find personal anecdotes sprinkled throughout my favorite recipes. These stories offer a glimpse into my heritage, the cultural significance of certain dishes, and the memories that have shaped my culinary path. To further enhance your cooking experiences, I've also included a comprehensive guide to essential spices. These aromatic treasures are the lifeblood of divine creation, unlocking a world of culinary possibilities.

Home cooking is essential for a healthy lifestyle. By preparing meals at home, you control ingredients, portions, and overall nutrition. Cooking demands intention, mindfulness, and heart. Infuse each dish with your soul, from ingredient selection to final plating. This mindful process nourishes both body and spirit. Join me on this exciting adventure in *Garden Exotica*.

Spice & Soul: A Global Feast from My Home Table

After living for a decade in the United States, I returned to Nepal in 2020 with a renewed sense of purpose. My desire was to reconnect with my roots, delve deeper into Nepali culture, and finish my first cookbook *Plant-Based Himalaya*. Despite its small size, Nepal is a spirited crossroads where people and ideas from all corners of the planet converge. Tourists flock to experience its ancient art, breathtaking mountains, and rich agrarian traditions—food being a central element. During this time, I hosted Nepali cooking classes for many international travelers. Sharing my culinary heritage ignited a passion for exploring flavors beyond my own borders.

This exploration wasn't entirely new territory. My mother's time cooking Indian cuisine had laid a foundation. Now, I ventured into the diverse worlds of the Turkey, Syria, Mexico, France, Tibet, Morocco, Nigeria, Japan, Thailand, and more. Every new spice, every unfamiliar ingredient, became a portal to a different culture. Food, beyond sustenance, became a bridge to understanding and appreciating the complex mosaic of human experience.

By 2022 I had settled in Pokhara with my husband and finished my first cookbook. Pregnant with our first child, I awaited my visa approval. We embraced the joys of Pokhara's lakeside cafes, offering an array of vegan and vegetarian delights—Nepali, Mediterranean, Indian, and more. Living in America had instilled a love for these cuisines, and their focus on vegetables and lighter textures often made them my go-to choices. As we enjoyed the lake and envisioned a second cookbook, our brainstorming sessions were fueled by sunshine and tea.

However, visa delays added significant stress—a period my supportive husband helped me navigate by focusing together on recipe development in our small apartment in Kathmandu. Months later, in April 2023, my visa finally arrived, necessitating a difficult and risky flight back to the States at thirty-four weeks pregnant.

Shortly after returning and welcoming our daughter, I was thrilled to receive a second cookbook offer from my publisher. Though challenging, the arrival of my daughter Saraswati (perhaps with her own cravings for global flavors) coincided with the pure joy of creating *Garden Exotica*. From the initial concept, she has been an inspiration. This book reflects a desire to explore new cuisines together, fostering a love for homegrown ingredients and balanced meals for the whole family. She delights in garden walks, savors fresh herbs, and eagerly awaits the end of recipe photo shoots, ready to sample the day's creations. She's a happy baby, content in her father's care while I conceive *Garden Exotica*.

This cookbook aims to inspire you: to cook enticing food spanning the continents, embrace the joys of homegrown produce, create healthy and satisfying meals, and prioritize the well-being of yourself and your loved ones. By nurturing both your body and soul through nourishing meals, you'll discover the joy of cooking as a form of self-care and a way to strengthen the bonds that enrich your life.

Let's explore the world of plant-based cooking, cultivate a connection with the earth, and create wholesome meals filled with love, tradition, and a touch of the exotic. Bon appétit! Buen provecho! Itadakimasu! Khana Kham!

The kitchen is the heart of my home. Here, I spend my days crafting healthy meals for my family, carefully curating my spice rack, and transforming homegrown herbs into flavorful oils and sauces. This is my sanctuary. Let me share my favorite kitchen rituals with you.

My Kitchen Essentials

POWER OF SEEDS & NUTS

Elevate your pantry with the simple ritual of toasting nuts and seeds. Once a month, take a moment to toast a variety of these flavorful ingredients. Store them in airtight containers to preserve their satisfying crunch, transforming them into versatile pantry staples. Enjoy them straight from the jar for a satisfying snack, or sprinkle them on top of dishes for a delightful taste bud explosion.

PUMPKIN SEED DELIGHT

For a special treat, transform your homegrown pumpkin seeds into a delightful snack! Simply wash the seeds, then carefully pick off any remaining pulp. Dry them on a tea towel and toss a drizzle of olive oil, a sprinkle of salt, and your favorite herbs. Spread the seasoned seeds on a baking sheet and bake at 300°F for 15–20 minutes on lower level. Listen closely—as they near completion, you'll hear them start popping like tiny firecrackers! Let the roasted seeds cool completely before enjoying them on their own or sprinkling them over recipes for an extra burst of flavor and texture. I use a muscat pumpkin from Nepal and their flavor is unique, reminiscent of a blend of soybeans and sesame. They are also incredibly crunchy.

TOASTING TIPS

While I prefer stove-top toasting for most nuts and seeds, the oven works well too. Here's a breakdown for each method:

STOVE TOP

Heat a dry skillet over medium heat. Add your chosen nuts or seeds. For walnuts, pecans, and pine nuts, stir frequently for 5–10 minutes.

Peanuts can be a bit tricky. Start with medium heat, then reduce to medium–low and watch closely, stirring constantly. You can add a teaspoon of olive oil for extra flavor. When you smell a nutty aroma, they're almost done (around 15–18 minutes). Let them cool completely on a flat plate before storing, as their crunch intensifies as they cool.

Sesame seeds are a bit different! Toast sesame seeds in a dry skillet over medium heat, stirring constantly with short breaks in between. Watch for the white sesame seeds to turn golden brown. Once sesame seeds start to pop, reduce heat to low and continue stirring constantly to prevent burning. This process can take up to 30 minutes for 3 cups of seeds. To test for doneness, grab a few seeds and rub them between your thumb and index finger. If they crumble and release a toasted aroma, they're ready. Place them on a flat plate to cool completely before storing or grinding for future use.
To unlock even more flavor possibilities, grind a few tablespoons of sesame seeds for a delightful addition to salad dressings, soups, pickles, or curries.

OVEN

Preheat your oven to 300°F. Spread your nuts or seeds on a baking sheet and bake for 10–15 minutes, stirring halfway through. Be watchful, as oven times can vary slightly for different nuts.

SYMPHONY OF AROMAS: *GARDEN EXOTICA*'S SPICE ODYSSEY

Imagine a bustling marketplace in Kolkata, India, the air heavy with the intoxicating scent of saffron, cardamom, and turmeric. Across continents, a wisp of smoke rises from a comal in Mexico City, carrying the pungent aroma of freshly toasted cumin, chilies, and black pepper. Spices, the silent storytellers of global cuisine, craft a captivating blend of fragrance and flavor that transcends borders and cultures.

My spice cabinet is a culinary globe-trotter, taking me on a flavorful journey without leaving home. Each spice carries tales of distant lands and food traditions. From the fiery embrace of chili peppers to the subtle warmth of nutmeg, these aromatic treasures transform ordinary ingredients into extraordinary dishes. My kitchen is a fragrant stage where spices perform their roles, creating a symphony of flavors. Be it the earthy depth of cumin or the citrusy brightness of coriander, these flavor profiles dance and intertwine, creating a unique taste experience.

Spices are more than just seasonings—they are the heart and soul of countless cultures. The art of grinding spices fresh unlocks a world of flavor. In *Garden Exotica*, we'll explore the endless possibilities that spices offer. Prepare to be transported around the world through the power of taste, as we savor the magic of spices in every recipe.

TIPS FOR THE CHEF

- *Invest in a spice grinder. Freshly ground spices release an explosion of aroma and flavor that preground options simply cannot match.*
- *Embrace the ritual of toasting spices like cumin and coriander seeds in a dry skillet. The warmth unlocks their essence, adding a deeper dimension to your dishes.*
- *Don't be afraid to experiment! Spices are a playground for creativity. Explore unexpected pairings and discover your own signature blends.*
- *Keep them in airtight containers away from light and heat to preserve their flavor.*
- *Taste as you go and adjust the amount of spices based on your preference.*
- *Build your spice collection gradually. Start with a few essential spices and expand your collection as you explore different cuisines from around the globe.*
- *Invest in high-quality spices for the best flavor.*
- *Create flavorful infused oils for a quick and easy way to add depth to your dishes.*
- *Grow your own herbs. Fresh herbs can elevate any dish and provide a constant supply of aromatic ingredients.*

From ancient healing remedies to modern-day gourmet creations, spices continue to inspire. Here is my ever-growing spice collection and the dishes I create with them.

HERBS & SPICES	ORIGIN	FLAVOR	DISHES
ALLSPICE PEPPER	Caribbean and Central America	Warm, spicy, with notes of cinnamon, nutmeg, and cloves.	Jerk sauce, pumpkin pie, pickling spices, curries.
ANISE	Middle East	Sweet, licorice-like flavor.	Tea, baked goods, sauce, curries, soups.
BASIL	Mediterranean	Sweet, slightly pungent and spicy.	Pesto, tomato sauce, salad, stir-fry.
BAY LEAVES	Mediterranean	Warm, bitter, with subtle notes of camphor and eucalyptus.	Curries, soup, stew, sauce. (I also use them as insect repellent)
BLACK PEPPER	India	Pungent, spicy, and earthy.	All cuisines.
BORAGE	Mediterranean	Cucumber-like and slightly salty taste with a hint of mint.	Garnish, infused oils, salads, drinks (lemonade, cocktails).
CALENDULA	Southern Europe	A blend of bitter and peppery notes with a touch of sweet citrus.	Tea, garnish salad and desserts, vinegars, infused oils for skincare.
CARDAMOM	India	Warm, sweet, floral with citrus notes.	Curries, tea, soup, desserts.
CAROM SEED	Middle East	Thyme-like, and slightly bitter.	Dal, curries, bread, vegetable fritters.
CHILI	South America	Spicy with fruity, earthy, and smoky undertones.	Any spicy dish.
CILANTRO	Mediterranean	Bright, citrusy, and herbaceous flavor.	Mexican salsa, curries, Indian and Nepali chutneys.
CINNAMON	Sri Lanka	Aromatic, warm, and subtly sweet.	Desserts, masala tea, curries, soups.
CLOVES	Indonesia	Pungent, slightly bitter, and floral with a touch of sweetness.	Vegetable rice, mouthwash, curries, tea.
CORIANDER SEEDS	Mediterranean	Citrusy, earthy, and slightly sweet when toasted.	Curries, Middle Eastern dishes, pickling.
CUMIN	Middle East	Warm, earthy, and slightly nutty flavor with a hint of bitterness.	Curries, stew, sauce, stir-fry
DILL	Mediterranean	Bright, fresh, and slightly pungent.	Pickled cucumbers, salad, soup, curries.
FENUGREEK	Mediterranean	Bitter, slightly acrid, and sweet flavor profile when cooked.	Curries, dal (soup), momo, salad.
GARLIC	Central Asia	Strong, pungent, and spicy.	All cuisines.
GINGER	Southeast Asia	Spicy, earthy, and aromatic.	All cuisines, tea, desserts.
JIMBU	Upper Mustang region of Nepal	Flavor reminiscent of onion and garlic.	Tempering soup (dal), vegetable curries.
MINT	Mediterranean	Fresh, cool, and slightly sweet.	Mojitos, salads, sauce.
BROWN AND YELLOW MUSTARD SEEDS	Himalayan region	Pungent with an intense, wasabi-like heat.	Curries, pickles, sauce.
NIGELLA	Middle East	Nutty, peppery, and onion-like.	Breads, spice blends, curries, stir-fry.
NUTMEG	Indonesia	Warm, sweet, and slightly spicy.	Soup, jerk sauce, desserts, hot beverage.
OREGANO	Mediterranean	Warm, slightly bitter, and earthy.	Pizza, pasta, tomato sauce, salads, soup.
PAPRIKA	Central Mexico	Earthy, slightly sweet, and pungent.	Curries, dips, tagines, sauce.
PARSLEY	Mediterranean	Bright, fresh, and slightly pungent.	Tabbouleh, chimichurri, soup.
PUL BIBER	Syria	Moderate heat, fruity and earthy.	Salads, dips, roasted vegetables, pasta.
SALT	Global	Mineral rich.	All cuisines.
SUMAC POWDER	Middle East	Tangy, citrusy, and slightly smoky.	Middle Eastern salads, garnish hummus.
TIMUR	Nepal	Citrusy, floral, and tingling sensation.	Nepali cuisine, tomato sauce.
THYME	Mediterranean	Woody, earthy, and slightly minty.	Sauce, stews.
TURMERIC	India	Warm, earthy, and a slightly pungent flavor reminiscent of mustard.	Curries, dal (soup), stir-fry, stew.

Sauces are the hidden gems of the kitchen, transforming simple ingredients into flavor explosions. Surprisingly easy to make, a single batch can elevate meals all week long. Delve into the world of fresh herbs: they add aromatic magic, and growing your own is incredibly rewarding.

SAUCE & DIP

Chimichurri

GARDEN-FRESH SAUCE: PERFECT FOR EVERYTHING

Chimichurri is ideal for marinating tofu, tempeh, or vegetables. Simply enjoy on crusty bread, or use it as a delicious sauce for salads, pasta, or pizza.

INGREDIENTS

½ cup finely chopped parsley
¼ cup finely chopped cilantro
2 cloves garlic
½ cup olive oil
½ teaspoon dried oregano
2 tablespoons red wine vinegar
¼ teaspoon red chili flakes
½ teaspoon black pepper
2 green chilies
½ teaspoon sea salt

Get ready to elevate your grilling game by marinating with this addictive chimichurri sauce!

Prep the Herbs: Wash the parsley and cilantro thoroughly. Pat them dry with a clean kitchen towel to remove excess moisture.

Finely Chop the Ingredients: Begin by finely mincing the garlic cloves. Next, finely chop the parsley, cilantro, and chilies.

Combine in a Bowl: Transfer the chopped garlic, herbs, and chili to a bowl.

Add Remaining Ingredients and Season: Pour in the olive oil, oregano, red wine vinegar, red chili flakes, black pepper, green chilies, and salt. Stir the chimichurri sauce well to combine all the ingredients. Taste and adjust the seasonings as needed. You can add more garlic for a stronger flavor if desired. Let it rest for at least 30 minutes to a few hours for the flavors to meld together.

Serve and Enjoy!

TIPS

- *SMOOTHER CHIMICHURRI: Pulse ingredients with olive oil in a food processor for a smoother texture before mixing in remaining ingredients by hand. Sometimes I add more water and less oil to cut down oil.*
- *STORAGE: Store leftover chimichurri in an airtight container in the fridge for 3–7 days. I also freeze them in ice cube trays for later.*
- *GROW YOUR OWN: Homegrown herbs often have a fresher flavor.*

Peanut Sauce

CREAMY & DREAMY: UNLOCK THE NUTTY GOODNESS

Consider using this sauce in your lachha paratha roll and for dipping vegetables, drizzling over noodles and rice bowls, or even as a base for other flavorful creations.

INGREDIENTS

1 cup roasted peanuts
1 clove garlic
1 tablespoon extra-virgin olive oil
1 tablespoon sesame oil
2 tablespoons lime juice
1 medium-size tomato, diced
1 small onion, chopped
2 tablespoons maple syrup
1 cup water
1 teaspoon salt

This creamy and rich peanut sauce is the perfect balance of sweet, salty, and savory.

Roast the Peanuts: Heat a cast-iron skillet over medium heat. Add the peanuts and stir them continuously. As the peanuts start to brown, reduce the heat to low and continue stirring frequently to prevent them from burning. Roast the peanuts for about 10 minutes or until they become golden brown and fragrant. To test if the peanuts are done, remove one from the pan and try cracking it open. If the skin comes off easily and the peanut has a slight crunch, the peanuts are fully roasted.

Cool the Peanuts: Remove the skillet from the heat and let the roasted peanuts cool for 10 minutes. Stir them occasionally as they continue to roast slightly from the residual heat of the pan. Once completely cool, the peanuts should be crisp.

Sauté the Aromatics: Heat olive oil in a separate pan over medium heat. Add the whole garlic cloves and sauté for about a minute, until fragrant. Add the chopped onion and cook for 2–3 minutes or until softened and starting to brown.

Simmer the Tomato Mixture: Add the diced tomato and salt to the pan with the onions. Stir to combine and cover the pan with a lid. Simmer over medium heat for 5 minutes. Remove the lid, stir the mixture, and use a spatula to crush the tomatoes slightly.

Cool the Tomato Mixture: Turn off the heat and let the tomato mixture cool completely.

Blend the Peanut Sauce: In a blender, combine the cooled tomato mixture, roasted peanuts, sesame oil, maple syrup, lime juice, salt, and water. Blend until smooth and creamy. Adjust the water to your preference.

Serve and Enjoy!

TIPS

- *STORAGE: Leftover peanut sauce can be stored in an airtight container in the refrigerator for up to 3 days.*
- *FRESHLY ROASTED FOR BEST FLAVOR: For the most flavorful peanut sauce, using freshly roasted peanuts makes a big difference. Store-bought roasted peanuts can lack the depth of flavor and satisfying crunch that come from home-roasting. Consider buying a large bag of raw peanuts and roasting them in batches throughout the month. This sauce can be a fun alternative to traditional pizza sauce.*

Cilantro Pesto

BEYOND BASIL: FRESH HERBAL FLAVORS FOR EVERY DISH

This pesto pairs well with pasta dishes and grilled vegetables/tofu or simply can be spread on toasted bread. I also add to soups, curries, noodles, salads, and dips.

INGREDIENTS

4 garlic cloves
6 oz (170 g) cilantro
½ cup olive oil
1 green chili
1 teaspoon sea salt
2 tablespoons lemon juice
1 tablespoon toasted pine nut (optional)

This recipe offers a fresh and flavorful alternative to traditional basil pesto, using cilantro as the star ingredient.

Clean the Cilantro: Wash the cilantro thoroughly and pat it dry with a clean kitchen towel.

Blend the Pesto: In a food processor, add the garlic cloves and blend for a few seconds until minced. Add the cilantro and blend again until finely chopped.

Add Remaining Ingredients and Blend: Pour in the olive oil, green chili, salt, lemon juice, and pine nuts (if using). Blend the mixture until you reach your desired consistency. For a smoother pesto, blend for a longer time.

Serve and Enjoy!

TIPS

- *GROW YOUR OWN: I grow cilantro at home for more delicious and aromatic cilantro pesto.*
- *REFRIGERATOR STORAGE: Store leftover pesto in an airtight container in the refrigerator with a drizzle of extra virgin olive oil on top to prevent browning. It will stay fresh for up to a week.*
- *FREEZER STORAGE: Cilantro pesto can also be frozen for longer storage. Freeze the pesto in an ice cube tray for individual portions or in a freezer-safe container. Once frozen, transfer the pesto cubes to a sealed bag.*

Marinara

GLOBAL PALATE, LOCAL GARDEN: HOMEMADE TOMATO SAUCE

This sauce is phenomenal over fettuccine pasta, as pizza sauce, with rice, or even as a delicious dip. Try it with some nachos for quick snacks.

INGREDIENTS

35 oz (990 g) sweet tomatoes
4 tablespoons olive oil
½ cup white onion, diced
6 cloves garlic, finely sliced crosswise
1¼ teaspoons sea salt
1 teaspoon paprika
½ teaspoon dried oregano
¼ teaspoon black pepper, coarse
1 teaspoon timur pepper powder
2 tablespoons ground sesame powder
1 oz (28 g) basil, chopped
¼ teaspoon baking soda (optional)

TIPS

- *TOMATO SELECTION: For the sweetest marinara sauce, using ripe tomatoes is key. Roma tomatoes, cherry tomatoes, and San Marzano tomatoes are all excellent choices due to their natural sweetness. I'm fortunate to grow my own cherry and San Marzano tomatoes at home for this purpose!*
- *BALANCING ACIDITY: While riper tomatoes create a naturally sweeter sauce, there are ways to work with less ripe tomatoes. This recipe uses baking soda as a way to slightly neutralize acidity and create a more balanced flavor. If you prefer a sweeter sauce, you can also add a touch of maple syrup or sugar to taste.*
- *TIMUR PEPPER: Sichuan pepper is the most widely recognized English name for Timur pepper in the market. It is readily available in Indian, Nepali, and Asian stores.*

Prep the Tomatoes: Wash the tomatoes thoroughly and cut them in half. Cherry tomatoes can be used whole.

Sauté the Onion: Heat a large saucepan over medium heat and add olive oil. Add the chopped onion and a pinch of salt. Sauté the onion for about 5 minutes over medium–low heat, stirring occasionally, until it becomes translucent. Avoid letting the onion brown too deeply.

Add Garlic and Tomatoes: Add the garlic and cook for an additional minute over low heat. Then, increase the heat to medium, add the tomatoes, and mix well.

Simmer the Sauce: Cover the saucepan with a lid, leaving a small gap for steam to escape. Simmer the sauce for about 20 minutes, stirring occasionally, until the tomatoes soften and release their juices.

Crush Tomatoes and Season: Remove the lid and use a spatula to partially crush the tomatoes. Season the sauce with remaining salt, paprika, oregano, black pepper, sesame powder, and timur. Stir well to combine all the ingredients.

Thicken the Sauce: Reduce the heat to medium–low and simmer the marinara uncovered, stirring occasionally, until it thickens to your desired consistency. This may take an additional 15–20 minutes depending on your choice of tomatoes.

Finish with Basil: Once the sauce has thickened, turn off the heat and stir in the chopped fresh basil. Allow the sauce to cool slightly as the basil infuses its flavor.

Blend the sauce (optional): Large tomatoes tend to have more juice and less skin, so blending them isn't usually necessary. However, blending cherry tomatoes after they've cooled will result in a smoother, more velvety sauce. If you're using the sauce for dipping, a thicker consistency is ideal. When using it with pasta or falafel, you might want to add a little water to thin it out to your preferred consistency.

Serve and Enjoy!

Mango Chutney

TROPICAL TWIST: THE SWEET HEAT SENSATION

Traditionally enjoyed with rice, roti, or samosas, mango chutney also pairs beautifully with bread and crackers. It can also be used as a dip for vegetables like carrot and celery.

INGREDIENTS

9 oz (255 g) green mango, deseeded
2 tablespoons olive oil
½ teaspoon fennel seeds
½ teaspoon nigella seeds
3 whole red chilies
¼ teaspoon cumin powder
¼ teaspoon turmeric
¼ teaspoon sea salt
3 oz (85 g) jaggery
1½ cups water

TIPS

- *JAGGERY: Jaggery is a natural sweetener made from unrefined cane sugar. Jaggery has a distinct flavor that is often described as molasses-like or caramel-like, with a hint of bitterness.*
- *CONSISTENCY: The amount of water you add will affect the final consistency of the chutney. Start with less water and add more if needed to achieve your desired texture.*
- *MANGO SELECTION: Use two large green (unripe) mangoes or several smaller ones. Since mangoes have a large central pit, adjust the number of mangoes accordingly to ensure you have enough usable fruit.*

Elevate your taste buds with this mango chutney, a perfect blend of sweet, spicy, and tangy.

Prep the Mango: Wash, peel, and cut the green raw mango into small cubes. Remove the pit.

Temper the Spices: Heat a saucepan over medium heat and add the oil. Add the fennel seeds, nigella seeds, and red chilies. Temper for a few seconds, until the fennel seeds become fragrant and start to turn light brown.

Cook the Mango: Add the chopped mango cubes, cumin powder, salt, and turmeric powder to the pan with the tempered spices. Stir well and cook for about a minute.

Simmer the Chutney: Cover the pan with a lid and simmer the mango mixture for 5 minutes. Reduce heat to medium–low if necessary to prevent burning.

Add Sweetener and Water: Add the water and jaggery (or brown sugar) to the pan. Stir well to combine and bring to a simmer. Cover the pan with the lid and cook for an additional 10 minutes, stirring occasionally, until the jaggery dissolves and is well incorporated into the mixture.

Adjust Consistency: Remove the lid and check the mixture. Continue cooking, stirring occasionally, until the mangoes soften and become mushy according to your desired consistency. For a smoother chutney, cook until the mangoes break down completely. For a chunkier chutney, cook until the mangoes are softened but still retain some texture.

Cool the Chutney: Once cooked, turn off the heat and let the chutney cool.

For Smooth Chutney: Transfer the chutney mixture to a blender and blend until smooth. Add few tablespoons of water if needed.

For Chunky Chutney: Enjoy the chutney without blending for a chunky texture with visible pieces of mango and spices.

Serve and Enjoy!

Caesar Salad Dressing

THE CREAMY CHAMELEON: A DAIRY-FREE DELIGHT

This dressing pairs perfectly with romaine lettuce for a classic Caesar salad, or enjoy it on any salad you like. It's also delicious on burgers, flatbread sandwiches, or even as a dipping sauce for fries.

INGREDIENTS

1 cup raw cashews
1 cup warm water
2 cloves garlic
2 tablespoons lemon juice
1 tablespoon capers
½ teaspoon salt
¼ teaspoon black pepper
1 tablespoon olive oil

This recipe offers a delicious and vegan alternative to traditional Caesar salad dressing, using cashews to create a creamy and flavorful base.

Soak the Cashews: In a bowl, cover the raw cashews with the warm water and soak for at least 30 minutes to 1 hour. Soaking softens the cashews and makes them blend smoothly.

Blend the Dressing: Add the soaked cashews and water to a blender along with the remaining dressing ingredients: lemon juice, garlic, capers, olive oil, salt, and black pepper. Continue blending the dressing ingredients until smooth and creamy. You may need to add a little extra water if the mixture is too thick.

Taste and Adjust: Taste the dressing and adjust seasonings as needed. Finish with a touch of lemon zest for extra brightness.

Serve and Enjoy!

TIPS

- *STORAGE: Leftover dressing can be stored in an airtight container in the refrigerator for up to 3 days.*
- *AVOIDING CAPER BRINE: When using capers, it's best to remove them from the jar with a utensil like a spoon or fork to avoid adding excess brine to your dressing. The strong vinegar flavor in the brine can overpower the other ingredients.*

Spicy Timur Sauce

MOUNTAIN MAGIC: FEEL THE ZING

This dressing pairs perfectly with romaine lettuce for a classic Caesar salad, or enjoy it on any salad you like. It's also delicious on burgers, flatbread sandwiches, or even as a dipping sauce for fries.

3 medium-size tomatoes
1 tablespoon sesame oil
½ teaspoon cumin seeds
¾ teaspoon sea salt
2 green chilies
1 cup cilantro, chopped
1 tablespoon perilla seed (silam)
½ teaspoon timur pepper powder (sichuan pepper)
1 teaspoon fresh lemon juice

Transform your tacos and more with this herbaceous, mouth-tingling homemade timur sauce. This sauce will awaken your palate and inspire you in the kitchen.

Roast the Tomatoes: Heat sesame oil in a pan over medium heat. Add cumin seeds and cook until they start to crackle and release their aroma. Cut the tomatoes in half and place them in the pan, cut-side down. Season with salt, mix gently, and cover the pan. Cook for 3 minutes, then carefully flip the tomatoes. Cover again and cook for several more minutes, until they are softened and slightly caramelized.

Toast Perilla Seeds: Toast perilla seeds over medium heat in an iron skillet, stirring constantly, about 5–7 minutes until fragrant and lightly golden brown. Be careful not to burn them. Once toasted, allow them to cool completely.

Blend the Sauce: In a blender, combine toasted perilla seeds, fresh cilantro, lemon juice, green chilies, and fragrant timur powder. Blend until smooth and creamy, adding water gradually, a tablespoon at a time, as needed to achieve your preferred consistency. I like mine thick and creamy.

Serve and Enjoy!

- *STORAGE: Leftover sauce can be stored in an airtight container in the refrigerator for up to 3 days.*
- *GROW YOUR OWN: Cilantro was a staple herb in my diet long before I delved into international cuisine. It remains one of my all-time favorites! I'm fortunate to grow my own cilantro in my garden, enjoying its fresh flavor from spring until the end of fall.*
- *SEED VARIATION: Perilla seeds can be easily found in Nepali stores or online. If you can't find them, sesame seeds work just as well.*

Tamarind Sauce

BEYOND SWEET & SOUR: THE TANGY TWIST

This delicious sauce is perfect for dipping, drizzling, and so much more! Try it with samosas, samosa chaat, or your favorite snacks and meals.

8 oz (226 g) sweet tamarind, no shell
2 cups water
1 oz (28 g) jaggery
4 whole red chilies
½ teaspoon cumin powder
½ tablespoon ginger, minced
1 tablespoon lemon juice
½ teaspoon sea salt

TIPS

- *STORAGE: Leftover tamarind sauce can be stored in an airtight container in the refrigerator for up to a week.*
- *SEEDLESS TAMARIND OPTION: For added convenience, seedless tamarind paste is also available in the market, saving time during sauce preparation.*
- *JAGGERY SUBSTITUTE: Jaggery, a type of unrefined cane sugar, adds a rich caramel flavor to the sauce. If you can't find jaggery, feel free to substitute it with regular sugar or brown sugar. Maple syrup can also work, although it will alter the flavor profile slightly.*

Indulge in the rich and complex taste of this homemade tamarind sauce, a culinary treasure.

Prep the Tamarind: There are two main types of tamarind available: sweet tamarind pods in shells and dried, deshelled tamarind (which is typically more sour). For this recipe, focus on finding sweet tamarind pods with shells.

Peel the shells off the tamarind pods and remove any large veins from the sticky pulp inside.

Simmer the Tamarind: Heat a saucepan over medium heat and add water. Bring the water to a boil, then reduce heat to low. Add the tamarind pulp and jaggery. Simmer for 20 minutes or until the tamarind pulp softens thoroughly.

Extract the Pulp: Turn off the heat and allow the tamarind mixture to cool completely. Once cool, use your hands to squeeze the tamarind pulp, separating the pulp and juice from the seeds and remaining veins. Discard the seeds and veins, leaving only the thick tamarind pulp in the saucepan.

Blend the Sauce: Transfer the tamarind pulp to a blender. Add the red chilies, salt, cumin powder, lemon juice, and ginger. Double check for any remaining seeds before blending. Blend until the sauce is smooth and velvety.

Serve and Enjoy!

Jerk Sauce

SPICY ISLAND VIBES: AN EXOTIC MARINADE

Jerk sauce is traditionally used to marinate meat and works exceptionally well with tofu, tempeh, or vegetables. For optimal flavor, marinate for at least a few hours, or ideally, overnight.

INGREDIENTS

1 large orange
1 habanero
2 cloves garlic
½ tablespoon ginger, minced
½ cup red onion, chopped
4 tablespoons olive oil
1 tablespoon maple syrup
5–6 sprigs fresh thyme
1 teaspoon sea salt
1 teaspoon nutmeg, freshly grated
1 teaspoon allspice pepper
3 green onions, roughly chopped

Jerk sauce is a truly unique condiment. Its blend of spices and aromatics results in a complex and flavorful sauce that can elevate any dish.

Prep the Ingredients: Peel the orange and gather all the remaining ingredients.

Blend the Sauce: In a food processor or blender, combine the orange, habanero, garlic, ginger, onion, oil, maple syrup, thyme leaves, salt, nutmeg, allspice pepper, and green onion. Blend until smooth.

Serve and Enjoy!

TIPS

- *CHILI OPTION: Traditionally jerk sauce is made with scotch bonnet pepper, but it is difficult to find in the stores, so feel free to add whatever spicy chili you have access to.*
- *STORAGE: Store leftover jerk sauce in an airtight container in the refrigerator for up to a week.*
- *TEXTURE VARIATIONS: Using a food processor can create a slightly chunkier texture in the jerk sauce compared to a blender, which will produce a smoother consistency.*
- *FRUITY VARIATIONS: This recipe uses orange for a citrusy touch. Feel free to experiment with other fruits like pineapple for a sweeter and more tropical flavor profile.*

Sunshine Yogurt Dip

HERB HEAVEN: RADIANT VEGAN YOGURT DIP

Perfect for everything from wraps and falafel to fresh vegetables, this creamy and bright herb yogurt dip is a light and refreshing addition to any picnic, beach day, or backyard barbecue.

INGREDIENTS

2 cups plant-based yogurt
2–3 tablespoons lemon juice
¾ teaspoon sea salt
2 cloves garlic, finely grated
½ cup white sesame seeds, toasted
1 medium-size cucumber, grated
1 tablespoon olive oil
1 teaspoon brown mustard seeds
¼ cup onion, thinly sliced
½ cup green peas
½ teaspoon lemon zest
1 tablespoon dill, finely chopped
1 teaspoon mint, finely chopped
1 teaspoon cilantro, finely chopped
½ teaspoon dried mango powder
¼ teaspoon pul biber for garnish
Few mint leaves for garnish
Freshly grated black pepper for garnish

This irresistible yogurt dip draws inspiration from tzatziki, raita, and chukauni, creating a delightful harmony of fresh herbs, tangy yogurt, and tender vegetables.

Combine Yogurt and Base: In a blender, combine the toasted sesame seeds, lemon juice, salt, and minced garlic. Pulse a few times to combine, then add the yogurt and blend until smooth and creamy.

Prep the Cucumber: Grate the cucumber and squeeze out any excess moisture with your hand or cheesecloth.

Fold in Herbs and Cucumber: Add the grated cucumber to the yogurt mixture. Gently fold in the chopped fresh dill and cilantro. Transfer the dip to a serving platter.

Temper the spices: Heat olive oil in a pan over medium heat. Add the mustard seeds and cook until they begin to pop and change color, releasing their aroma. Add the chopped onion and cook for several minutes, until softened and golden brown. Stir in the green peas, lemon zest, and a pinch of salt. Mix well and cook for 3–4 minutes, or until the peas are tender and vibrant green. Spoon the fragrant tempering over the prepared yogurt dip. Garnish generously with dried mango powder, pul biber, fresh mint, dill, and black pepper.

Serve and Enjoy!

TIPS

- *HERB VARIATIONS: Dill is the key herb in this recipe, but feel free to experiment with other fresh herbs to suit your taste preferences.*
- *SOUR ADJUSTMENT: Don't be afraid to add a little extra lemon juice or pomegranate molasses to your sauce! Vegan yogurt isn't as sour as dairy-based yogurt, so you may need a bit more to get the perfect tang.*

Mint Chutney

EAST MEETS MINT: REFRESH YOUR SENSES

Mint chutney is a total game-changer! Its unique flavor is amazing with crispy samosas or pakoras, and it adds a fresh element to vegan curries and dips.

INGREDIENTS

2 cups fresh mint leaves
1½ tablespoons lemon juice
1 jalapeno chili
¼ teaspoon sea salt
2–3 tablespoons water
1 tablespoon olive oil
1 tablespoon toasted peanuts (optional)
2 small fire-roasted tomatoes (optional)

From appetizers to main courses, this mint chutney adds a burst of flavor and aroma to any dish.

Prep the Mint: Wash the mint leaves and remove any thick stems.

Blend the Chutney: Combine mint leaves, lemon juice, chili, olive oil, and salt in a blender. Blend until smooth.

Adjust Consistency: If the chutney is too chunky, add water. Only add 1 tablespoon at a time, until you reach your desired consistency.

Serve and Enjoy!

TIPS

- *MINT VARIETIES: Feel free to experiment with different types of mint, such as chocolate mint, peppermint, or spearmint to create unique flavor variations.*
- *TRADITIONAL TWIST: For authentic flavor, grind the fire-roasted tomatoes with mustard oil and mint in a mortar and pestle. This method maximizes smokiness and umami, creating my preferred taste profile.*
- *GROW YOUR OWN: For those fortunate enough to have a garden; spearmint, curly mint, and even pineapple mint can thrive in perennial gardens. This offers a readily available source of fresh mint for your culinary creations.*

Smoky Eggplant & Bell Pepper Dip

KISSED BY FIRE: DIP, SPREAD, DEVOUR

Enjoy this smoky dip with veggies, warm pita, or toasted sourdough. Its versatility makes it a perfect addition to any gathering, from casual weeknight meals to lively parties.

INGREDIENTS

1 big red bell pepper (capsicum)
1 large or 2 medium-size eggplants
1 tablespoon pomegranate molasses
2 cloves garlic
1 red chili
1 tablespoon olive oil
½ teaspoon sea salt

TIPS

- *POMEGRANATE TWIST: For an extra layer of fruity tartness, drizzle in some pomegranate molasses to taste after blending. Keep a jar of pomegranate molasses in your refrigerator—it's a versatile ingredient that elevates dips and salads.*
- *CREAMY VARIATION: Add a touch of creaminess by incorporating a few tablespoons of toasted walnuts or sesame seeds to the blender with the other ingredients.*
- *SIMILAR RECIPE: This dip is similar to eggplant bharta, but the addition of red bell pepper and pomegranate molasses creates a unique flavor profile.*

Looking for a delicious and easy appetizer that's sure to impress? This smoked eggplant and bell pepper dip is a winner! It's simple to make, packed with flavor, and perfect for serving with pita bread, vegetables, or crackers.

Roast the Vegetables: Prepare the grill for direct heat. Place the whole eggplant and red bell pepper directly over the coals. Roast, turning occasionally, until softened and blistered. The eggplant will typically take 10–15 minutes, while the bell pepper will be ready in 5–8 minutes. Alternatively, preheat your oven to 425°F (220°C). Cut the eggplant in half, place the pieces in a baking pan with garlic. Drizzle with oil, and sprinkle with salt. Roast for about 30 minutes, or until tender. I roast the garlic until golden for about 10–15 minutes, then remove it from the oven to cool while the eggplant continues cooking.

Cool and Peel: Once roasted, transfer the vegetables to a plate and let them cool completely. Once cool, the charred skin of the grilled vegetables should peel away easily. Discard the stems and tops of the eggplant and pepper. If you are using the oven method, there's no need to peel the skin.

Blend the Dip: In a blender, combine the roasted eggplant, bell pepper, molasses, garlic, chili, olive oil, and salt. Blend until smooth, scraping down the sides as needed. For a thinner consistency, add a tablespoon or two of water while blending.

Serve and Enjoy!

Roasted Tomato Guacamole

GUAC WITH A CHARRED KISS: SMOKY, SWEET, SUBLIME

Indulge in the classic pairing of this dip with crisp tortilla chips. For a heartier option, savor it with corn tortillas brimming with grilled vegetables or a succulent red kidney bean burger.

INGREDIENTS

3 ripe avocados
3 medium tomatoes, fire roasted
¼ cup red onion, chopped
½ cup cilantro, chopped
1 tablespoon fresh lime juice
⅛ teaspoon black pepper, coarse
1 serrano chili, finely chopped
1 teaspoon sea salt

TIPS

- *AVOCADO PREP: Gently hold the avocado in the palm of one hand. With the other hand, use a sharp knife to cut lengthwise around the seed. Twist the halves apart. Gently tap the pit with the knife blade and twist to remove it. Or, use a spoon to scoop out the seed.*
- *NO FIRE, NO PROBLEM: To grill your tomatoes, cut them in half and place them on a hot grill for approximately 5 minutes, or until cooked through.*

This unique twist on classic guacamole combines the richness of avocados with the smoky sweetness of roasted tomatoes.

Roast the Tomatoes: There are two options for roasting the tomatoes:

Fire Method: If using a charcoal grill, build a small fire. Place the tomatoes directly over the heat source and roast for about 5 minutes per side or until the skins are charred and the tomatoes are softened.

Stovetop Method: Place the stovetop grill on a medium heat burner. Roast the tomatoes directly on the grill for approximately 3 minutes per side, or until charred and softened.

Cooling and Storing: Once roasted, transfer the tomatoes to a plate and let them cool completely. The charred skin will peel away easily. Discard the peeled skins and roughly chop the tomatoes. Any leftover roasted tomatoes can be stored in an airtight container in the refrigerator for up to 3 days.

Mash the Tomatoes: In a large bowl, use a fork to mash the roasted tomatoes. If any areas of the tomato flesh weren't fully softened during roasting, you can use a knife to finely chop those pieces.

Assemble the Guacamole: Cut the avocado in half, remove the pit, and use a spoon to scoop the avocado into chunks and add to a bowl. Combine the mashed tomatoes and all remaining ingredients: red onion, cilantro, lime juice, serrano chili, black pepper, and salt. Gently fold the ingredients together until combined. Taste the guacamole and adjust seasonings with additional salt or lemon juice as desired. Garnish with chopped fresh cilantro.

Serve and Enjoy!

Pumpkin Hummus

FALL FLAVORS BLOOM: DIP INTO HARVEST

Easy to whip up and bursting with autumnal goodness, this pumpkin hummus is a must-try.

INGREDIENTS

2 cups pumpkin, washed and peeled
4 tablespoons olive oil
1 cup chickpeas, boiled
3 tablespoons tahini
3 tablespoons fresh lemon juice
2 cloves garlic
7 tablespoons water
½ teaspoon sea salt
¼ black pepper, coarse
½ teaspoon cumin powder
¼ teaspoon red chili powder
Sumac powder for garnish

TIPS

- *TAHINI RECIPE: Combine a cup of home-roasted white sesame seeds, a pinch of sea salt, and 1 tablespoon of olive oil in a blender. Blend, gradually adding 3-4 tablespoons of olive oil in 1-tablespoon increments, until the mixture becomes smooth. Store extra tahini in the refrigerator.*
- *CHICKPEA OPTIONS: For canned chickpeas: Drain, rinse, and cook for 15 minutes before adding to the blender. For dried chickpeas: Soak overnight. Drain, rinse, and cook in an Instant Pot on high pressure with a pinch of salt and baking soda for 6 minutes. Let the chickpeas cool completely before adding to the blender.*
- *ADD CRUNCH: For an added crunch, garnish with toasted pine nuts, toasted sesame seeds, or walnut.*
- *STORAGE: Leftover roasted pumpkin can be stored in an airtight container in the refrigerator for up to 4 days.*

This pumpkin hummus is a taste of fall in every bite—creamy, flavorful, and incredibly satisfying.

Preheat the Oven: Preheat your oven to 400°F (200°C). Line a baking sheet with parchment paper.

Marinate the Pumpkin: Remove the outer skin and the seeds/strings from the inside. Then cut the pumpkin into 2-inch-thick slices. In a bowl, toss the pumpkin slices with 1 teaspoon of olive oil, salt, black pepper, cumin powder, and red chili powder. Let the pumpkin marinate for 15 minutes while the oven preheats.

Roast the Pumpkin: Spread the marinated pumpkin slices in a single layer on the prepared baking sheet. Roast in oven for 40 minutes or until the pumpkin is tender and easily pierced with a fork.

Cool the Pumpkin: Remove the roasted pumpkin from the oven and let it cool completely.

Blend the Hummus: In a blender, combine the roasted pumpkin, chickpeas, tahini, lemon juice, garlic, and water. Blend until smooth and creamy, scraping down the sides as needed. This may take about 2 minutes.

Adjust Consistency: With the motor running, slowly drizzle in additional water, 1 tablespoon at a time, until the hummus reaches your desired consistency.

Serve and Enjoy: Transfer the hummus to a shallow dish or serving bowl. Drizzle with olive oil and sprinkle with sumac powder for a tangy touch and visual appeal.

Cashew Cream Cloud Dip

MELT-IN-YOUR-MOUTH GOODNESS: EASY, CHEESY, BEAUTIFUL

Enjoy rich and satisfying meals with this versatile and delicious dairy-free alternative. Use it to elevate lasagna, salads, sandwiches, charcuterie, and pasta.

INGREDIENTS

½ cup raw cashews
1 cup warm water to soak cashews
1 tablespoon lemon juice
2 teaspoons nutritional yeast
2 tablespoons coconut oil
½ teaspoon sea salt
½ teaspoon garlic powder
1 tablespoon apple cider vinegar
1 tablespoon tapioca flour (optional)

This recipe is entirely vegan and dairy-free, but it delivers a satisfyingly cheesy flavor with a touch of umami.

Soak the Cashews: Rinse the cashews. Transfer them to a bowl and cover them with warm water. Soak the cashews for at least 30 minutes, or up to 2 hours, to soften them.

For Dip: Add cashews, nutritional yeast, lemon juice, coconut oil, garlic powder, apple cider vinegar, and salt to a blender. Gradually add water while blending until smooth and creamy. Serve immediately or refrigerate in an airtight container for a few hours.

For Pizza: Add all ingredients, including the soaking water and tapioca flour to a blender. Blend until completely smooth. Transfer the mixture to a small saucepan and cook over low heat, stirring continuously, for approximately 5 minutes, or until the mixture thickens and develops a slightly stretchy consistency. Remove from heat and use immediately on pizza or store in an airtight container in the refrigerator for later use.

Serve and Enjoy!

TIPS

- *MOZZARELLA MAGIC: This cloud dip surprisingly resembles mozzarella cheese in both texture and appearance. When shaped and chilled for at least 30 minutes, it can even be sliced. For a golden color and fragrant flavor, I sometimes add a pinch of saffron.*
- *TAPIOCA TOUCH: A touch of tapioca flour helps the cashew cream achieve a delightful golden brown crust when briefly cooked. Sometimes I add 1–2 tablespoons of tapioca to the cashew blend to create a cheese-like texture.*
- *FAST AND FUSS-FREE: The best part? This recipe comes together quickly, making it perfect for busy weeknights. Plus, unlike store-bought vegan cheese, you know it's additive-free.*

Salads take center stage in *Garden Exotica*. Transform your salads into stunning meals with fresh, homegrown ingredients. Discover inspiring recipes, from summery light bites to hearty main courses. Let's dive in!

SALAD

Green Mung Bean Bulgur Salad

WHERE GARDEN MEETS GRAIN: A SYMPHONY OF FLAVORS

The light and refreshing flavors of the Mung Bean Bulgur Salad are perfectly complemented by a satisfying Pumpkin Hummus sandwich, offering a delightful contrast in textures and temperatures.

INGREDIENTS

1 cup yellow bulgur, coarse
1½ cups water for cooking bulgur
½ cup green mung bean, whole
2 cups water for soaking mung beans
1½ teaspoons salt
2 tablespoons pomegranate molasses
½ cup parsley, finely chopped
¼ cup green onion, finely chopped
1 tablespoon holy basil, finely chopped
¼ cup lemon juice, freshly squeezed
1 small red beet, grated
½ teaspoon black pepper, freshly ground
Handful of fresh pomegranate
¼ cup pistachios, chopped for garnish
A few borage flowers for garnish

TIPS

- *SPICE IT UP: Feel free to adjust the fresh herbs and spices to your liking.*
- *JUST A STARTING POINT: This salad is delicious on its own or can be used as a filling for tacos or dumplings.*
- *MUNG BEAN PREP: Avoid overcooking the mung beans to prevent them from becoming mushy.*
- *GO NUTS: Substitute other nuts for the pistachios, if desired.*

Craving something fresh and nutritious? Try this Mung Bean Bulgur Salad, bursting with earthy flavor and nutty texture.

Prepare the Mung Beans: Place mung beans in a shallow bowl. Rinse thoroughly under cold running water (3–4 times). Cover with 1 cup of water and soak for at least 6 hours, or preferably overnight.

Cook the Mung Beans: Transfer soaked mung beans with water to a saucepan. Add fresh water if needed to cover them by about an inch. Add ½ teaspoon of salt. Bring the water to a boil over medium heat. Reduce heat to medium–low and simmer for about 12 minutes or until the mung beans are tender. Drain the cooked mung beans and set them aside to cool.

Cook the Bulgur: Bring water to a boil in a saucepan. While the water heats, rinse the bulgur thoroughly under running water. Once the water boils, add the rinsed bulgur in the pan. Reduce heat to medium–low and cook for about 8 minutes, stirring occasionally, until the bulgur is cooked through and the water is absorbed. Remove the bulgur from the heat and spread it out on a flat plate to cool.

Prepare the Dressing and Combine: In a large mixing bowl, whisk together the pomegranate molasses, parsley, green onion, holy basil, lemon juice, grated beets, salt, and black pepper.

Assemble the Salad: Add the cooled bulgur to the dressing and mix well to coat. Incorporate the cooked mung beans and gently fold them into the salad. Let the salad rest for 5–10 minutes to allow the flavors to meld. Garnish your mung bean bulgur salad with fresh pomegranate, chopped pistachios, and borage flowers.

Serve and Enjoy!

Spicy Sesame Noodle Salad

SESAME SIZZLE: SPICY PASTA SALAD WITH A BITE

Fabulous on its own or take it up a notch as fresh Asian summer spring rolls. Fill rice paper wrappers with the salad, sliced cucumber, fresh herbs like mint or basil, and a drizzle of peanut sauce.

INGREDIENTS

14 oz (396 g) extra firm tofu, diced
2 tablespoons olive oil, for frying tofu
2 tablespoons ginger, crushed
¼ teaspoon black pepper
3 tablespoons lime juice
2 tablespoons sesame oil
3 tablespoons toasted black sesame seeds
1½ teaspoons salt
½ cup red cabbage, thinly sliced
½ cup red onion, thinly sliced
¼ cup green onion, chopped
½ cup carrot, julienne
¼ cup red bell peppers, thinly sliced
2 green chilies, chopped
½ cup cilantro, finely chopped
½ cup roasted peanuts
5 oz (140 g) linguine pasta
1 fresh lime

TIPS

- *TOASTED NUT: For a delightful textural contrast, consider toasting peanuts, sesame seeds, or your favorite nuts at home. Store them in an airtight jar for easy access when assembling recipes.*
- *SPICE LEVEL: Control the spiciness of the salad by adjusting the amount of green chili pepper.*
- *STORAGE: Leftovers can be stored in an airtight container in the refrigerator for a day or overnight.*

Impress your guests with this showstopping Spicy Sesame Noodle Salad that is as delicious as it is beautiful.

Marinate the Tofu: Drain the water of the tofu, pat it dry with a clean kitchen towel, and gently press to remove excess moisture. Cut the tofu into cubes and place them in a mixing bowl. Crush fresh ginger using a mortar and pestle, then add to the bowl with ½ teaspoon salt, black pepper and 1 tablespoon of lime juice. Gently toss to coat the tofu evenly. Let the tofu marinate for 15–30 minutes at room temperature.

Make the Sesame Dressing: Grind 2 tablespoons of black sesame seeds. Reserve 1 tablespoon of the toasted sesame seeds for garnish. In a separate bowl, whisk together the ground sesame seeds, 1 tablespoon of sesame oil, 1 tablespoon of lime juice, and 1 teaspoon of salt.

Prepare the Vegetables: In a large bowl, combine the cabbage, sliced red onion, green onion, julienned carrot, bell pepper, green chilies, and chopped cilantro. Pour the sesame dressing over the vegetables and toss to coat. Let the salad marinate for 10 minutes.

Cook the Pasta: Bring a large pot of salted water to a boil. Add the linguine pasta and cook about 8–10 minutes, or until al dente. Drain the pasta in a colander and rinse briefly under cold water. Drain thoroughly. Toss the pasta with 1 tablespoon of sesame oil and set aside to cool.

Fry the Tofu: Heat a flat skillet or cast-iron pan over medium heat. Add oil. Fry the marinated tofu cubes for 2–3 minutes per side or until golden brown and crispy. Adjust the heat as needed to prevent burning. Transfer the cooked tofu to a plate and let it cool slightly.

Assemble the Salad: Add the cooled linguine pasta to the bowl of salad. Gently fold all ingredients together with two wooden spoons. Add the tofu cubes and toasted peanuts, then fold again to combine. Transfer the salad to a serving bowl and garnish with the reserved toasted black sesame seeds, chopped green onion, and a squeeze of fresh lime juice.

Serve immediately and enjoy!

Biwaz / Onion & Parsley Salad

PARSLEY POWER: REFRESHING AND BRIGHT

A classic falafelball hoagie or wrap is the perfect complement to this onion and parsley salad. For a lighter option, enjoy it alongside a grilled vegetable sandwich.

INGREDIENTS

1 red onion, thinly sliced
Handful of parsley, chopped
1 teaspoon sumac powder
1 teaspoon red wine vinegar
1 teaspoon olive oil
⅛ teaspoon of salt

This onion salad is a twist on a classic childhood dish, I enjoyed with rice, curries, and wraps. Adding parsley, red wine vinegar, and sumac powder took the flavor profile to a whole new level!

Prepare the Onions: Wash and pat dry the red onion. Slice the onion thinly lengthwise and then again into thin strips. Place the sliced onion in a bowl.

Combine and Marinate: Add the chopped parsley, olive oil, red wine vinegar, salt, and sumac powder to the bowl with the onions. Toss well to coat all ingredients evenly. Let the salad rest for 10 minutes to allow the flavors to meld.

Serve and Enjoy: Biwaz is best enjoyed fresh, while the onions retain their crisp texture.

TIPS

- *HERB VARIATIONS: I love incorporating fresh dill and cilantro from my herb garden when it's in season. Feel free to experiment with other herbs you enjoy.*
- *ADJUST TO YOUR TASTE: Don't hesitate to adjust the amount of red wine vinegar and seasonings to suit your preferences. If you don't have red wine vinegar you can add lemon juice.*
- *STORAGE: Leftover Biwaz salad can be stored in an airtight container in the refrigerator for up to 24 hours. Be aware that the onions may soften slightly over time.*

Black-Eyed Pea Salad

SOUTHERN COMFORT: A HARVEST OF HERITAGE

A colorful broccoli stir-fry with carrot and snap peas perfectly complements the black-eyed pea salad or expand your mezze with dips like smoky eggplant and pepper dip or tzatziki.

INGREDIENTS

1 cup black-eyed peas, dried
2 cups water
1 stalk of romaine lettuce, chopped
1 medium tomato, diced
½ yellow bell pepper, diced
Handful of chives, chopped
A few stalks of cilantro, chopped
¼ teaspoon black pepper, freshly ground
1 teaspoon salt
1 teaspoon fresh lemon juice
Handful of pineapple mint for garnish
A few dandelions for garnish (optional)

Black-eyed peas are a staple food in many cultures around the world, including Nepali and American cuisine. Enjoy protein-packed peas tossed with fresh vegetables and a touch of cool mint.

Soak the Beans: In a large bowl, rinse 1 cup of dried black-eyed peas 2–3 times. Cover with 2 cups of water and soak for at least 8 hours, or preferably overnight.

Cook the Beans: Transfer the soaked beans to a saucepan and add fresh water to cover by about 2 inches. Add 1 teaspoon of salt. Cover the pan and bring the water to boil over high heat, then reduce heat to medium and simmer for 20–25 minutes or until the beans are tender but still hold their shape. Drain the cooked beans in a colander and set them aside to cool slightly.

Assemble the Salad: In a large bowl, combine black-eyed peas with lettuce, tomato, bell pepper, chives, cilantro, black pepper, and salt. Drizzle with olive oil and lemon juice to taste. Toss gently to combine all ingredients. Garnish the salad with fresh mint leaves and serve immediately.

Serve and Enjoy!

TIPS

- *CUSTOMIZE YOUR SALAD: Adjust the amount of vegetables and herbs to your liking. I sometimes add boiled corn for extra sweetness and creaminess.*
- *SOAKING TIP: I soak black-eyed peas in the morning to cook in the evening or overnight to cook the next day.*

Strawberry & Walnut Salad

SPRINGTIME IN A BOWL: FRUITS & NUTS IN HARMONY

Enjoy this juicy salad on its own for a light and refreshing lunch, or as the perfect side dish to any savory dish in this book.

INGREDIENTS

10 oz (284 g) fresh strawberries
2 small cucumbers
2 celery stalks
1 cup spinach
½ cup toasted walnuts
Pinch of salt
Freshly ground black pepper
1 teaspoon olive oil (optional)
Handful of blueberries (optional)

TIPS

- *NUTRITIONAL BENEFITS: This salad is a nutritional powerhouse, packed with essential vitamins, antioxidants, and healthy fats. Spinach is an excellent source of vitamins A and K, while strawberries offer a boost of vitamin C and fiber. Walnuts contribute omega-3 fatty acids, beneficial for heart health.*
- *STORAGE: Leftover salad can be stored in an airtight container in the refrigerator for up to 24 hours. While the freshness will be maintained, the texture of the spinach may soften slightly.*

This easy-to-make salad is a family favorite! Sweet strawberries, crunchy walnuts, and a refreshing mix of cucumber, celery, and spinach make it a delightful treat. Even my toddler can't resist!

Toast the Walnuts (optional): If you haven't toasted the walnuts yet, heat a cast-iron skillet over medium heat. Add the walnuts and toast for 5–8 minutes, stirring constantly, until golden brown and fragrant. Be careful not to burn them. Set aside to cool slightly on a plate.

Prepare the Salad: Wash and chop all the ingredients to bite size, keeping the strawberry slices larger for a satisfying, juicy crunch.

Assemble and Toss: In a large bowl, combine the spinach, strawberries, walnuts, salt, and a hint of black pepper. Toss gently to coat all ingredients evenly.

Add Blueberries (optional): For an extra burst of flavor and antioxidants, feel free to add a handful of fresh blueberries.

Serve and Enjoy!

Tempeh Caesar Salad

BURSTING WITH RICHNESS: A TASTE OF VEGAN PARADISE

A rustic sourdough would provide an irresistible base for this salad sandwich. The crisp lettuce, creamy dressing, and savory tempeh adding a delicious crunch and flavor.

INGREDIENTS

4 oz (113 g) fresh romaine leaves
8 oz (226 g) tempeh
2 tablespoons maple syrup
2 small habanero peppers
4 cloves garlic
2 tablespoons olive oil
½ teaspoon salt
½ teaspoon freshly ground black pepper

Sauce
Caesar Salad Dressing (page 30)

TIPS

- *CRISP LETTUCE: Wash the romaine lettuce thoroughly. For optimal crispness, pat it dry with a clean cotton towel and store it in the refrigerator. Remove the lettuce just before assembling the salad.*
- *SPICE IT UP: Adjust the amount of habanero pepper to your desired level of heat. Add the Caesar dressing gradually, tossing after each addition to achieve the perfect level of dressing for your taste.*

A delightful combination of textures and flavors awaits in this salad. It features marinated tempeh with a kick, creamy Caesar dressing, and crisp romaine lettuce. A delicious and satisfying vegan twist on the classic Caesar salad!

Steam the Tempeh: Boil water in a steamer. Wash and place tempeh inside the steamer and steam for 10 minutes. Let it cool slightly to absorb flavor. Cut the cooled tempeh into ½-inch wide strips and place in a mixing bowl.

Marinate the Tempeh: In a mortar and pestle (or blender), grind the habanero pepper and garlic. Add the ground mixture, maple syrup, salt, and black pepper to the bowl with the tempeh. Toss well to coat and marinate for at least 1 hour in the refrigerator.

Cook the Tempeh: Heat a pan over medium heat and add olive oil. Once the oil is hot, add the marinated tempeh strips in a single layer. Cook for 3 minutes per side or until golden brown and crispy. Transfer the cooked tempeh to a plate to cool slightly.

Chop and Drizzle the Lettuce: Wash and dry lettuce on a kitchen towel. Chop the lettuce into bite-sized pieces (or use whole baby romaine leaves if preferred). Toss the chopped romaine with ½ cup of Caesar dressing.

Serve and Enjoy: Transfer the salad to a serving platter. Add the cooled and crispy tempeh strips to the salad bowl and gently fold everything together. Top with additional Caesar dressing and a sprinkle of freshly cracked black pepper, if desired.

Potato & Avocado Salad

GREEN GOODNESS & TATERS : NATURE'S PERFECT PAIRING

Enjoy this rejuvenating salad alone or piled high on your favorite bread. The crunch of cucumber and sunflower seeds adds a delightful texture and makes it a perfect lunch.

INGREDIENTS

3 medium potatoes
3 tablespoons olive oil
¾ teaspoon sea salt
¼ teaspoon black pepper, freshly ground
1 cucumber, diced
2 avocados, pitted and diced
2 tablespoons fresh lemon juice
½ cup cilantro, chopped
1 teaspoon parsley, finely chopped
Handful of toasted sunflower seeds
Half lime for drizzle

This dreamy salad combines creamy avocado, crispy potatoes, and refreshing cucumber for a delightful side dish. It's the kind of salad that everyone loves, and it's perfect for any occasion.

Cook the Potatoes: Place the potatoes in a saucepan and cover them with water. Bring the water to a boil over high heat. Reduce heat to medium and simmer for 30 minutes or until the potatoes are fork-tender.

Drain and Cool: Drain the cooked potatoes in a colander and let them cool completely. Cut the potatoes into medium cubes.

Fry the Potatoes: Heat a pan or cast-iron skillet over medium heat and add olive oil. Once the oil is hot, add the cubed potatoes. Fry the potatoes for 5–7 minutes per side or until golden brown and crispy. Season with salt and black pepper, then transfer the fried potatoes to a bowl to cool slightly.

Assemble the Salad: In a large bowl, combine diced cucumber, avocado, lime juice, chopped cilantro, parsley, and a pinch of salt. Gently toss. Add cooled fried potatoes and fold gently.

Serve and Enjoy: Transfer to a serving platter. Garnish the salad with toasted sunflower seeds and fresh cilantro leaves. Enjoy!

TIPS

- *CUSTOMIZE YOUR SALAD: Feel free to adjust the amount of lime juice and seasonings to suit your taste preference.*
- *NUTTY VARIATION: For a richer flavor, try using toasted pecans or walnuts instead of sunflower seeds.*

Taro Root Salad

FROM THE EARTH: A ROOT VEGETABLE DELIGHT

A bowl of basmati rice alongside sweet potato and peanut soup would create an enticing base for the taro root salad, offering a complete and nutritious meal.

10 oz (283 g) taro root
1 tablespoon olive oil
⅛ teaspoon sea salt
1 tablespoon lemon juice
1 stalk celery, sliced
1 medium tomato, diced
5–7 pitted black olives
Handful of red onion, sliced
Handful of parsley, chopped

Taro root is a versatile root vegetable with a slightly earthy flavor. It's a staple food in many cultures around the world, including Nepal. While traditionally cooked in stews or dals, taro root can also be enjoyed in salads like this one.

Prepare the Taro Root: Clean the taro root by rubbing it with a damp kitchen towel to remove any dirt. Alternatively, wash and let it dry overnight. Peel the skin from the taro root using a sharp knife or peeler. Cut the peeled taro root into bite-sized chunks. Avoid washing it under running water immediately before cooking, as this can make the taro root slimy and difficult to cut.

Cook the Taro Root: Place the taro root chunks in a large saucepan and cover them completely with water. Bring the water to a boil over high heat. Reduce heat to medium and simmer for 10–12 minutes or until the taro root is tender when pierced with a knife. Drain the cooked taro root and set it aside to cool slightly. Alternatively, you can also steam taro root for about 15 minutes until tender.

Make the Dressing: In a small bowl, whisk together olive oil, salt, and lemon juice to create a simple vinaigrette.

Assemble the Salad: In a large mixing bowl, combine the cooled taro root, celery, tomato, black olives, red onion, and parsley. Pour the prepared vinaigrette over the salad ingredients and toss gently to coat everything evenly.

Serve and Enjoy! Transfer the salad to a serving platter and share with your loved ones.

- *CUSTOMIZE YOUR DRESSING: Feel free to adjust the amount of lemon juice and salt in the dressing to suit your taste preference.*
- *PREPPING TARO ROOT: For easier handling, break the taro root into large chunks after peeling. Then cut the boiled chunks into bite-sized pieces for the salad.*

Butter Bean Garden Salad

FESTIVE GREENS: A SWEET & SAVORY MEDLEY

This garden delight is a zesty burst of flavor, perfect for summer picnics or a refreshing addition to any dish from the cookbook.

INGREDIENTS

½ cup butter beans, dried
3 cups water
1 small kombu
1 tablespoon pomegranate molasses
¼ cup cilantro, finely chopped
1 medium carrot, shredded
1 medium beet, grated
Handful of mixed greens
¼ cup roasted pine nuts
½ cup fresh pomegranate
1 tablespoon olive oil
¼ teaspoon sea salt

This celebration salad features protein-rich butter beans tossed with sweet beets, tangy pomegranate seeds, and crunchy pine nuts. Kombu, a type of seaweed, adds a subtle depth of flavor and helps make the beans more digestible.

Soak the Beans: Rinse dried butter beans and place them in a large bowl. Cover them with 3 cups of water and soak overnight. The beans will expand significantly during soaking, so be sure to use a large bowl.

Cook the Beans with Kombu: Transfer the beans to a saucepan and add water to cover them completely. Add salt, a 2-inch piece of kombu seaweed on top. Bring the water to a boil over high heat. Reduce heat to medium, cover the pan with a slightly ajar lid (to allow steam to escape), and simmer for 45 minutes or until the beans are tender but still firm. Alternatively, cook them in an Instant Pot on high pressure settings for 10 minutes with all the water and salt. Allow for a natural pressure release for 20 minutes before carefully releasing any remaining pressure.

Remove the kombu seaweed. You can chop it finely and add it to the salad, or save it for future soups. Drain the cooked beans and let them cool slightly.

Sauté Beans (Optional): Heat a pan with oil. Add the beans and salt. Sauté and cook in medium heat for 10 minutes, stirring occasionally. When golden brown, turn off the heat and let them cool.

Make the Dressing: While the beans cool, prepare a simple dressing in a large bowl. Whisk together pomegranate molasses and fresh cilantro.

Assemble the Salad: Add the cooled beans to the dressing and toss to coat. In a bowl, combine chopped kombu, beets, carrots, mixed greens, and pomegranate. Gently toss to combine. Let the salad rest for 5 minutes to allow the flavors to meld.

Serve and Enjoy: Finish the salad with a pinch of salt and toasted pine nuts for a delightful buttery flavor.

TIPS

- *SIMPLE DRESSING OPTION: For a quicker dressing, simply omit the molasses and use olive oil, salt, fresh lemon juice, and black pepper to taste.*
- *NO KOMBU? NO PROBLEM: If you don't have kombu seaweed, you can still cook the butter beans without it.*
- *COOKING TIPS: Butter beans can be tricky to cook, often requiring long cooking times and potentially developing an unpleasant odor if improperly prepared. My preferred method is the Instant Pot for consistent and quick results. The skins often slip off naturally after cooking, and removing them creates a smoother texture. For convenience, you can also use a 15 oz can of butter beans. If you can't find butter bean, use great northern bean instead.*

Nepal's "dal," a comforting lentil soup, is a staple of my heritage. This chapter expands beyond my childhood favorites to explore a global array of soups, from nourishing lentil stews to robust broths. Discover the warmth and flavor simmering in pots around the world.

SOUP

Peanut & Sweet Potato Stew

SUNSHINE IN A POT: A COLORFUL & FLAVORFUL CREATION

A bed of fluffy rice (white, brown, basmati, or even wild rice) is a classic pairing. It soaks up the flavorful stew beautifully.

INGREDIENTS

1½ cups peanuts, roasted
3 cups water
¼ cup parsley, chopped
1½ teaspoons salt
3 tablespoons olive oil
4 cups sweet potatoes, ½-inch diced
⅔ cup onion, diced
½ red pepper (capsicum), diced
1 teaspoon ginger, minced
1 teaspoon garlic, minced
2 teaspoons cumin powder
2½ cups tomatoes, diced
1 cup baby spinach leaves

TIPS

- *ADJUST THE CONSISTENCY: For a thinner stew, simply add more water or vegetable broth.*
- *SPINACH SUBSTITUTE: You can use kale or another leafy green. Just be sure to chop the greens before adding them to the stew.*
- *STORAGE: Leftovers can be stored in an airtight container in the refrigerator for up to 3 days. Reheat gently over low heat.*
- *INSTANT POT CREATION: Craving a comforting and hassle-free meal? Simply add all the ingredients, including the peanut sauce, to your Instant Pot. Set it to high pressure for 6 minutes, and you'll have a delicious bowl of soul in no time.*

This comforting stew features tender sweet potatoes simmered in a rich peanut sauce, brightened with pops of red pepper and spinach.

Toast the Peanuts: Heat a cast-iron skillet over medium heat. Add the peanuts and toast them, stirring frequently, for 10–15 minutes or until golden brown and fragrant. Be careful not to burn the peanuts. Reduce heat if necessary. Transfer the toasted peanuts to a plate to cool completely.

Make the Peanut Sauce: Combine the toasted peanuts, ½ teaspoon of salt, parsley, and water in a blender or food processor. Blend until smooth and creamy.

Sauté the Vegetables: Heat olive oil in a large pot or Dutch oven over medium heat. Add the onion and red bell pepper, stirring occasionally for 2–3 minutes or until softened. Add the diced sweet potatoes and cook for an additional minute. Close the lid and cook over medium–low heat for 10 minutes, stirring occasionally.

Add Spices: Add the ginger and garlic paste along with the remaining salt and cumin powder to the pot. Combine well and cook for another minute, allowing the flavors to release. Close the lid and cook in medium heat for 5 more minutes or until the sweet potatoes are tender. Add tomatoes and mix well. Close the lid and cook for 10 minutes.

Finish the Stew: Add the peanut sauce to the stew and stir well. Add extra salt if needed. Return to a simmer and cook over medium–low heat for 10 more minutes or until the sweet potatoes are fully cooked. Stir in the fresh spinach and cook for about a minute. Remove the stew from the heat.

Serve and Enjoy!

Fava Bean Soup

EARTHY & DELIGHTFUL FLAVORS: A BOWL OF COMFORT

Serve this soup hot with warm and crusty bread, such as khobz, for dipping. It's a perfect dish for a chilly evening.

INGREDIENTS

1 cup fava beans, dried
4 cups water
4 oz (113 g) potatoes, peeled
1½ tablespoons olive oil
3 dried red chilies
½ cup onion, thinly sliced
1 tablespoon garlic, crushed
1 tablespoon ginger, crushed
6 cloves
1 teaspoon cumin powder
1 teaspoon coriander powder
½ teaspoon cardamom powder
1½ teaspoons salt
½ teaspoon red chili powder
2 cups tomatoes, diced
1 tablespoon pomegranate molasses
Handful of cilantro, chopped
A few chives (optional)

TIPS

- *RICHER FLAVOR: Use vegetable broth instead of water for the beans.*
- *STOVETOP (NO INSTANT POT): Soak beans overnight, then simmer 1 hour on the stovetop in medium heat until tender before continuing with the recipe.*
- *STORAGE: Store in an airtight container in the fridge for up to 3 days. Reheat gently.*

Inspired by Moroccan Bissara, this flavorful soup features protein-packed fava beans simmered in a fragrant tomato broth with potatoes and spices. It's a delicious and comforting dish, perfect for a cozy night.

Soak the Beans: Rinse 1 cup of dried fava beans and place them in a large bowl. Cover them with 4 cups of water and soak overnight.

Cook the Beans (Instant Pot): Transfer the beans to your Instant Pot along with the water, potatoes, and ½ teaspoon of salt. Close the lid and cook on high pressure for 10 minutes. Let the pressure release naturally for 20 minutes, then carefully release any remaining pressure.

Sauté the Aromatics: Heat olive oil in a large saucepan or Dutch oven over medium heat. Add dried chili peppers and cook for a few seconds, until fragrant. Add the chopped onion and cook for 2–3 minutes or until softened. Add ginger and garlic. Cook for an additional minute. Add the cloves, cumin powder, coriander powder, cardamom powder, salt, and red chili powder to the pan. Stir to coat and cook for 10 seconds, allowing the spices to release their aroma. Pour in the diced tomatoes and stir well. Bring to a simmer and cook for 5 minutes, until the tomatoes are soft.

Combine and Simmer: Add the potatoes, cooked fava beans, and molasses to the tomato mixture. Using a potato masher or fork, partially mash some of the fava beans and potatoes to create a thicker consistency. Add more water as needed for your preferred thickness. Once the soup boils, reduce the heat to low and simmer for 15 minutes.

Serve and Enjoy: Remove the soup from heat and stir in the fresh chopped cilantro and chives. Taste and adjust seasonings. Enjoy this flavorful soup hot, with a drizzle of olive oil if desired.

Thukpa

THE COZY CLASSIC: A TASTE OF HOME

Spicy, tangy, and soulful; this chickpea noodle soup is pure comfort in a bowl. Perfect for a cold day in your pajamas.

INGREDIENTS

3 tablespoons olive oil
1 tablespoon ginger, thinly sliced
2 cloves garlic, minced
2" whole cinnamon stick
5 oz (140 g) red onion, thinly sliced
1 bell pepper (capsicum), thinly sliced
5 oz (140 g) carrot, thinly sliced
5 oz (140 g) cabbage, thinly sliced
½ cup green peas
1 red chili, chopped
½ teaspoon timur powder
2 tablespoons sesame powder
1½ teaspoon salt
1 big tomato, diced
¼ cup cilantro, chopped
1 large lemon
3 oz (85 g) spaghetti (optional)

Homemade Noodle
1½ cups (226 g) wheat flour
1 cup (170 g) all purpose flour
½ cup corn flour for dusting
1½ teaspoon sea salt
220 mL (15 tablespoons) water
6 cups water for cooking

TIPS

- *VEGGIE VARIATIONS: Feel free to customize the vegetables! Try zucchini, green beans, broccoli, bok choy, or spinach for something different.*
- *NOODLE OPTIONS: This soup is best with thick noodles such as spaghetti or traditional Tibetan noodles.*
- *INSTANT POT TIP: If you are feeling lazy, put all the ingredients in the instant pot and cook in pressure cooker settings for 5 minutes. Use thin noodles like angel hair pasta to avoid overcooking.*

Experience the essence of Nepali Thukpa with this aromatic soup. Protein-rich green peas, a medley of tender vegetables, and springy noodles simmer in a fragrant, flavorful broth.

Prepare the Noodle: Mix flour and salt. Gradually add water and knead for about 10 minutes until a smooth dough forms. Cover the dough with a damp cloth and let it rest for 1–2 hours. Dust a work surface with cornflour, roll the dough to approximately 1–2 mm thickness, sprinkle with cornflour, fold twice, and slice into fine noodles (about 2 mm) using a sharp knife. Heat 6 cups of water until it simmers, then lower the heat to medium. Add the noodles and cook for 2–3 minutes, or until al dente, depending on their size. Remove the noodles using a mesh strainer and rinse them with cold water for a few seconds. Set aside the noodle water for the soup. You can also use a pasta machine to make the noodles, or use store-bought spaghetti as a substitute.

Sauté the Vegetables: In a large saucepan or Dutch oven, heat olive oil over medium heat. Add ginger and garlic, sautéing until fragrant. Stir in a cinnamon stick, red onion, and bell pepper, cooking for a minute. Add cabbage, green peas, carrots, and red chilies. Season generously with timur pepper, sesame powder, and salt. Combine thoroughly, then add tomatoes and chopped cilantro. Cover and cook for 2 minutes. Pour in the reserved noodle water, bring to a boil, then reduce heat to low and simmer for 5 minutes, or until the vegetables are tender. Remove from heat.

Serve and Enjoy: Ladle the steaming vegetable soup into two bowls. Add the desired portion of cooked noodles. Garnish generously with chopped cilantro. Squeeze the juice of a ripe lemon over each bowl, then gently combine. Serve immediately and relish this invigorating, mouth-tingling soup.

Store leftover soup and noodles in the refrigerator for your next meal.

Yellow Lentil & Pumpkin Soup

CREAMY SPICED DAL: EDIBLE AUTUMN

A bowl of this steaming soup pairs perfectly with a side of timur fries and fragrant cumin rice, creating a comforting and flavorful Nepali meal. Homemade pita bread is also a delicious addition.

INGREDIENTS

½ cup split piegon peas (toor dal), dried
½ cup split chickpeas (chana dal), dried
4 cups water for soaking
18 oz (510 g) pumpkin, diced
1½ tablespoons olive oil
1 teaspoon cumin seeds
2 dried red chilies
¼ cup onion, finely chopped
1 teaspoon ginger, finely chopped
1 green chili, finely chopped
1 tablespoon dried fenugreek leaves
¼ teaspoon turmeric powder
1 teaspoon sea salt
½ cup coconut milk
2 tablespoons cilantro, finely chopped
2 carrots, sliced (optional)
1 cup pumpkin, diced (optional)

TIPS

- *NO PUMPKIN? NO PROBLEM: The soup is delicious without pumpkin, so feel free to omit it. Feel free to substitute any seasonal vegetable you like.*
- *STOVETOP OPTION: In a shallow pot, combine the soaked lentil, pumpkin, and 4 cups of water. Simmer over medium heat until tender (30-40 minutes). Stir in the prepared tempered spices. Simmer for 10 minutes to allow the flavors to infuse, adding more water if necessary.*

Experience the delightful interplay of textures in this robust soup. Tender pumpkin, nutrient-dense split chickpeas and pigeon peas simmer in a fragrant coconut milk broth, while the optional roasted pumpkin and carrot topping adds an extra layer of umami and textural contrast.

Soak the Lentils: Combine both lentils in a large bowl and rinse 2–3 times under running water. Add 4 cups of water and soak overnight or for a minimum of 4 hours.

Cook the Lentils and Pumpkin (Instant Pot): Add the soaked lentils, soaking water, and the pumpkin to the Instant Pot. Add salt. Seal the Instant Pot and cook on high pressure for 6 minutes. Allow the pressure to release naturally for 20 minutes, then carefully release any remaining pressure manually.

Temper the Spices: As the lentils depressurize, prepare the tempering. Heat olive oil in a pan over low heat. Add cumin seeds and dried red chili peppers. Cook a few seconds until fragrant. Turn the heat to medium. Add the chopped ginger and onion. Cook for 3–4 minutes, or until softened and golden brown. Stir in the fenugreek leaves, green chilies, and turmeric. Cook for a few more seconds to release their aromas.

Combine and Simmer: Quickly stir the lentil soup into the pan with the tempered spices (tadka). Add coconut milk and season with salt to taste. Let it simmer for a few minutes, allowing the flavors to meld together.

Roasted Vegetable Topping (Optional): Preheat oven to 425°F (220°C). Toss additional pumpkin and carrots with olive oil, salt, and black pepper. Roast 30–35 minutes or until tender and browned. When serving the soup, sprinkle the roasted vegetables on top as a delicious and flavorful garnish. Alternatively, blend all ingredients for a smooth-textured soup.

Serve and Enjoy: Put the soup in a bowl, garnish with finely chopped fresh cilantro and enjoy.

Tom Yum Soup

EXOTIC VEGAN BROTH: A TANGY ESCAPE

Serve the steaming hot and fragrant Tom Yum soup with the cool, fluffy comfort of white rice and the crispy, juicy delight of zucchini tempura.

INGREDIENTS

2 tablespoons olive oil
4 dried red chilies
6 oz (170 g) shiitake mushrooms, sliced
1 cup red onion, sliced
½ cup tofu, diced
2 cloves garlic
1 stalk lemongrass
4 cups water
3 small slices galangal (optional)
2 tablespoons lime juice
2 lime leaves, hand crushed
2 medium tomatoes, diced
1 tablespoon maple syrup
1½ teaspoons salt
Handful of enoki mushrooms
½ cup coconut milk

TIPS

- *NO MORTAR AND PESTLE? Simply crumble or chop the dried chili pepper by hand before adding it to the coconut milk.*
- *SPICE IT UP: Adjust the amount of chili pepper to your desired spice level.*
- *MISSING GALANGAL OR LIME LEAVES? No problem! Substitute with extra lime juice and zest for a similar flavor. Lemongrass is a key ingredient for authentic Tom Yum, so try to include it if possible.*
- *VEGETARIAN TWIST: Traditionally made with seafood, this recipe offers a delicious vegan alternative. Feel free to add more mushrooms, greens, and other veggies.*

This sublime vegan Tom Yum soup features a intoxicating broth bursting with citrus, spice, and savory mushrooms. It's a light yet satisfying meal, perfect for a healthy dinner.

Sauté the Aromatics: Heat olive oil in a large pot over medium heat. Add the dried red chilies and cook for a few seconds, until fragrant. Remove the chilies with a spoon and set aside on a plate. Add the sliced shiitake mushrooms to the pot and cook for 3 minutes or until golden brown. Stir in the onion and tofu. Cook for an additional minute.

Release the Flavors: On a chopping board, use a pestle to crush the garlic cloves and lightly bash the lemongrass stalk. Add the crushed garlic and lemongrass to the pot with the vegetables and cook for one more minute.

Build the Broth: Pour in 4 cups of water and add the galangal, lime juice, lime leaves, maple syrup, enoki mushrooms, chopped tomatoes, and salt. Bring the soup to a boil. Add more water if you'd like a thinner broth, a little at a time, until the desired consistency is reached.

Coconut and Spice: In a mortar and pestle (or using a small blender), grind the reserved dried chili peppers into a paste. Add the coconut milk and chili paste to the simmering soup, stirring well. Reduce heat to low and simmer for 10 minutes.

Serve and Enjoy: Taste the soup and adjust the flavors with additional lime juice, salt, or maple syrup to your preference. Serve hot!

Great Northern Bean & Dill Soup

DREAMY DILL-ICIOUS: WARM YOUR SOUL WITH EVERY SPOONFUL

This soup works well in all seasons. Serve it hot with a hearty sandwich in the winter to warm you from the inside or chill it in the summer to beat the heat.

INGREDIENTS

1 cup great northern beans, dried
4 cups of water
1 teaspoon salt
½ cup chopped dill
1 tablespoon vegan butter
1 teaspoon jimbu
1 tablespoon lemon juice
1 teaspoon olive oil to drizzle on top
¼ cup lightly roasted pine nuts
A few cilantro flowers (optional)
Freshly grated black pepper for garnish

TIPS

- *FRESH DILL SUBSTITUTE: No fresh dill? Substitute 1 tablespoon dried dill but be aware the flavor will be less intense.*
- *JIMBU SUBSTITUE: Jimbu is an aromatic Himalayan herb with a distinct garlic-onion flavor. Look for it at Nepali stores or online. If you can't find jimbu, you can create a similar flavor base by sautéing chopped onion and garlic until lightly golden.*
- *COOL IT DOWN: For a refreshing twist, chill the soup for at least an hour before serving.*

Soak the Beans: Rinse the beans thoroughly and place them in a large bowl. Cover the beans with 4 cups of water and let them soak overnight (at least 8 hours).

Cook the Beans: Transfer the soaked beans, soaking water, and salt to the Instant Pot. Secure the lid and cook on high pressure for 6 minutes. Allow a natural pressure release for 20 minutes, then carefully release any remaining pressure.

Toast the Nuts: Toast the pine nuts in a dry skillet over medium heat until fragrant (about 5 minutes). Set aside to cool.

Temper Jimbu: In a pan over medium heat, melt vegan butter. Add the jimbu and temper it for a few seconds, until it becomes fragrant and slightly golden. Add the tempered jimbu to the Instant Pot with the cooked beans. Stir in the chopped dill and mix well. Use a ladle to mash a few beans against the side of the pot to thicken the soup. Let the flavors meld.

Blend the Soup (optional): Transfer the soup to a blender. While blending, add water gradually to achieve your desired consistency.

Serve and Enjoy: Season with freshly ground black pepper to taste. Ladle the warm soup into bowls over a bed of fluffy rice. Garnish each serving with a drizzle of extra virgin olive oil, a squeeze of fresh lemon juice, a sprinkle of toasted pine nuts, sprigs of fresh dill, and delicate cilantro flowers.

While baking wasn't a part of my childhood, making flatbreads daily for my family cultivated love for the magic of bread. This chapter of *Garden Exotica* is my opportunity to explore the wonderful world of baking alongside you, sharing quick and easy recipes that bring those delicious breads back to your table.

BREAD

Dill Aaloo Paratha

SAVORY & SATISFYING: THE ALLURING POTATO-HERB FLATBREAD

Serve hot parathas with spicy timur sauce and your favorite yogurt dip for a delicious and phenomenal meal. Perfect for breakfast, lunch, or dinner!

INGREDIENTS

For Filling

4 medium-size potatoes
1.5 oz (42 g) fresh dill, chopped finely
½ cup red onion, finely chopped
1 teaspoon ginger, finely chopped
2 cloves garlic, finely chopped
1 green chili, finely chopped
1 teaspoon cumin powder
1 teaspoon salt
¼ teaspoon turmeric
Handful of cilantro, finely chopped

For Dough

4 cups whole wheat flour (atta)
¼ cup wheat flour for dusting
1 teaspoon olive oil
½ teaspoon salt
1½ cups water + 2 tablespoons

Sauce

Spicy Timur Sauce (page 32)
Sunshine Yogurt Dip (page 38)

TIPS

- *PERFECT POTATO TEXTURE: Aim for tender potatoes without going mushy. This ensures a good filling consistency.*
- *DRY GREENS, HAPPY FILLINGS: Squeeze out any excess moisture from the chopped greens to prevent a soggy filling. Also, make sure the potatoes are completely cooled and dry. A dry potato mixture will make your rolling easier without any breaks.*
- *CRISPY PERFECTION: The ideal paratha is crispy and golden brown. Adjust the cooking time slightly based on your pan and heat source to achieve this.*

Flaky layers of paratha envelop a flavorful filling of spiced potatoes and fresh dill in this irresistible Dill Aaloo Paratha.

Cook the Potatoes: Place the potatoes in a shallow pan and cover completely with water. Bring to a boil over high heat, then reduce heat to medium and cook for 30–35 minutes or until tender. Drain the water and let the potatoes cool completely.

Make the Filling: While the potatoes cool, combine dill, onion, ginger, garlic, green chili, cumin powder, turmeric, and salt in a mixing bowl. Mix well and let it rest while you prepare the dough.

Prepare the Dough: In a separate bowl, whisk together flour and salt. Add the oil and mix until crumbly. Gradually add water, kneading until a soft dough forms. Knead for 5 minutes, adding extra water by the tablespoon if needed to achieve the right consistency. Cover the dough with a plate and let it rest for 15–30 minutes.

Mash the Potatoes: Once potatoes are cool enough to handle, peel and mash the potatoes with a fork. Avoid over-mashing, leaving some texture. Leave out any large potato chunks that could tear the dough when rolling.

Combine Filling and Rest: Add the mashed potatoes to the spice mixture and gently combine. Let the filling sit for an additional 5 minutes to allow the flavors to meld.

Divide the Dough: Divide the dough into seven equal balls.

Follow the wrapping and cooking instructions on the next page.

Paratha

Layers of Flavor

Paratha, meaning "layered bread," is popular across the Indian subcontinent, typically enjoyed for breakfast or lunch. It can be plain, with added spices or stuffed with a variety of vegetables. Having grown up near the border of northern India, I experienced a delicious fusion of Nepali and North Indian cuisine. Plain paratha, layered with dough and ghee (clarified butter) and cooked on a flat iron skillet, was a staple in our household. Roti, another flatbread, was a regular part of our meals, while paratha was more of a weekend treat due to the extra ghee it required.

A Tradition Passed Down

Aloo paratha was a staple in my childhood. My mother, who ran a cold store in Kathmandu, would turn leftover small potatoes into delicious dishes like this. It was her specialty, and by the time I was twelve, I'd learned the art of making aloo paratha myself. I had a natural knack for cooking, and there was immense satisfaction in recreating my mother's recipes. I was so proud when I mastered the technique of folding and rolling the paratha dough without tearing. Looking back, I'm so grateful to my mother for these lessons—the importance of cooking and the joy of homemade food.

Growing up, we rarely ate out, except for the occasional momos (dumplings). Our meals were prepared at home, a tradition I cherish to this day. While aloo paratha is readily available in most Nepali and Indian restaurants, I highly recommend making it at home. The difference is night and day–fresh, flavorful, and not greasy.

Family Favorite

Aloo paratha, meaning "potato flatbread" in Nepali and Hindi, is a beloved street food enjoyed throughout Nepal and India. But it's more than just street fare—it's a versatile dish that can be served for breakfast, lunch, or dinner.

My time living in America has inspired me to create new ways to enjoy homemade flatbreads, like my unique and flavorful wrap recipe, which you won't find anywhere else. For me, dill aloo paratha is the ultimate comfort food. I love the fresh flavor dill brings, especially when it's grown in my own garden. It adds a special touch to parathas, fried rice, pide, pesto, chimichurri, and many other dishes. For a delicious variation, try substituting cilantro. You can also experiment with other fillings like radish, fenugreek leaves, cauliflower, or onion.

How to Roll Paratha

1. **Roll the Dough:** On a lightly floured surface, roll out each dough ball into an 8–9-inch circle.

2. **Add Filling:** Place a generous spoonful (4–5 tablespoons) of filling in the center.

3. **Fold the Dough 1:** Fold the dough sides over the filling, enclosing it completely.

4. **Fold the Dough 2:** Sprinkle some flour on the work surface and on top of the dough. Lightly press and flatten the filled dough ball with your hand.

5. **Roll the Filled Dough:** Gently roll out the filled dough into an 8–9-inch diameter. Add a little extra flour on both sides if needed to prevent sticking.

6. **Cook the Paratha:** Heat a flat pan or griddle over medium heat. Add a teaspoon of oil to the pan. Carefully place the paratha on the pan and cook for about 2 minutes. Drizzle another teaspoon of oil over the top and gently flip the paratha. Cook for another 2 minutes or until golden brown and crispy on both sides. Repeat with remaining dough and filling.

1
2
3
4
5
6

Lachha Paratha

CRISPY & FLAKY: LAYERS OF DELIGHT

Serve hot with your favorite chutney, curry, or vegetable stir-fry. Lachha Paratha is best enjoyed fresh from the pan! I love making lachha rolls.

INGREDIENTS

2 cups whole wheat flour (atta)
½ cup olive oil
¾ cup water + 2 teaspoons
1 teaspoon nigella seed
¼ teaspoon salt

TIPS

- *METHOD MAGIC: This recipe offers a user-friendly approach to creating lachha paratha. While other techniques exist, this one delivers a delicious and achievable result.*
- *SEED YOUR SUCCESS: Feel free to adjust the amount of nigella seeds to suit your taste preference. For a unique flavor, try substituting carom seeds.*
- *STORAGE: Leftover lachha paratha can be stored in an airtight container at room temperature for up to 24 hours or in the fridge for 3 days. To reheat, simply warm them in a pan with a little oil until crispy and heated through.*

Lachha Paratha is a beloved Indian flatbread, featuring irresistible crispy, flaky layers. This recipe offers a simple method for achieving that delightful flakiness.

Make the Dough: In a mixing bowl, combine flour, salt, and nigella seeds. Make a well in the middle, add 2 teaspoons of oil, and mix. Gradually add room-temperature water. Knead until a soft, slightly elastic dough forms. The dough should be soft but not sticky. Knead for 5 minutes and cover the bowl with a plate. Let it rest for 15–30 minutes.

Shape the Dough Balls: After the dough has rested, knead it a few more times on a lightly floured surface. Divide the dough into five equal portions, shaping each into a smooth ball. Keep the dough balls covered with a cloth or plate while you work to prevent them from drying out.

Roll the Dough: On a lightly floured surface, take one dough ball and roll it out into an 8–9-inch circle. If the dough feels sticky, sprinkle with a little more flour.

Create the Flaky Layers: Brush the entire surface of the rolled dough with 1 teaspoon of oil (I use my finger tips). Using a sharp knife, carefully make a straight cut from the center to one side of the outer edge.

Coil and Flatten: Gently pick up a corner of the dough and tightly roll it inward toward the opposite edge, starting from the middle of the circle. This will form a pinwheel-shaped coil resembling a cone. Gently press down on the pointed tip of the coil to flatten it into a disc. Use your fingers to further flatten the disc into a round patty shape. Sprinkle some flour and roll the dough with a rolling pin to a 7–8-inch diameter round.

Cook the Paratha: Heat a wide pan or griddle over medium heat. Add 1 teaspoon of oil. Once hot, carefully transfer the paratha to the pan. Cook for about 2 minutes. Add another teaspoon of oil around the edges and in the middle of the paratha. Flip the paratha with a flat spatula. Gently press on the edges and middle while cooking for another 2 minutes, or until golden brown and crispy on both sides. For extra flakiness, drizzle with a little more oil. Adjust the heat as needed to prevent burning. Repeat the process with the remaining dough balls.

Serve and Enjoy: Transfer the cooked paratha to a plate and enjoy while it is warm.

Lachha Paratha Wrap

HEALTHY & HEAVENLY: TASTE THE RAINBOW OF FLAVOR

The layers of flavor in this Lachha Paratha wrap are so delightful, you might just find yourself licking your fingers. Pair it with your favorite dipping sauces for an even more exquisite experience.

INGREDIENTS

3 tablespoons olive oil
1 teaspoon ginger, minced
1 clove garlic, minced
½ cup red onion, chopped
A few green chilies, finely chopped
18 oz (510 g) potatoes, boiled
¼ teaspoon turmeric
¾ teaspoon sea salt
2 cups fresh fenugreek leaves, chopped

For toppings
1 yellow bell pepper, thinly sliced
2 sweet red peppers, thinly sliced
1 small carrot, julienned
A few green onions, chopped
Handful of purple cabbage, finely chopped
Handful of cilantro, chopped

Sauce
Peanut Sauce (page 22)

TIPS

- *SPICE IT UP: Adjust the green chilies to your preferred spice level.*
- *BELL PEPPER BONANZA: Play around with any color combination you like, or omit them completely.*
- *FRESH OR DRIED FENUGREEK: If you don't have fresh fenugreek leaves, substitute dried leaves, easily found in Indian grocery stores or online.*
- *FILLING VARIATION: Feel free to get creative! Crumbled tofu, tempeh, green peas, baked eggplant, and other cooked vegetables make delicious alternatives to potatoes. Adjust seasonings to your liking.*

The aromatic flavor of fenugreek leaves shines through in the spiced mashed potato filling of these crispy lachha paratha wraps. Topped with colorful bell peppers, purple cabbage, and a drizzle of peanut sauce, they're a truly mouthwatering and indulgent meal.

Boil the Potatoes: Wash the potatoes. Place them in a large pot and cover completely with water. Bring to a boil over medium–high heat, then reduce heat to medium and simmer for about 30 minutes or until the potatoes are tender. You can check if they're done by poking them with a knife—it should go through easily. Drain the cooked potatoes and set them aside to cool completely. You can cut the potatoes in half to speed the cooling process.

Sauté the Aromatics: Heat a skillet over medium heat and add olive oil. Once hot, add ginger, garlic, green chilies, and onion. Sauté for 3–4 minutes or until golden brown and fragrant.

Mash and Add Potatoes: Using a fork, lightly mash the cooled boiled potatoes. Alternatively, you can break them up with your hands. Add the potatoes to the pan with the sautéed aromatics and stir well to combine.

Season and Cook: Season the mixture with turmeric and salt. Cook for an additional minute, allowing the flavors to meld.

Incorporate Fenugreek: Increase the heat to medium–high and add the fenugreek leaves. Cook for 5 minutes, stirring occasionally to prevent sticking and ensure even cooking.

Cool the Filling: Once cooked, turn off the heat and let the filling cool slightly.

Assemble the Wraps: Spread a generous portion of the potato filling onto a lachha paratha. Lightly layer sliced peppers, purple cabbage, cilantro, and green onions over the filling, arranging them like pizza toppings for a colorful presentation. Drizzle generously with peanut sauce.

Roll and Enjoy: Roll the paratha tightly, enclosing the filling and toppings. Cut the wrap in half and serve with additional peanut sauce for dipping.

Flatbread: Simple, Versatile, and Endlessly Delicious

From the comforting rotis of my Kathmandu childhood to the satisfying gyros of my college days, flatbreads have always held a special place in my heart. Growing up in Nepal, unleavened wonders like roti, paratha, and puri were the foundation of our meals. Their soft, slightly chewy texture is perfect for scooping up flavorful curries and stews. Leavened breads were a rarity, a world away from our daily breadbasket.

Moving to America introduced me to the magic of yeast-risen breads. During my college years, international cuisine was a treat, and gyros were a campus staple. I have vivid memories of those soft, fluffy pitas, bursting with savory meat, crisp vegetables, and tangy tahini sauce. It was a cheap, delicious, and filling meal that was perfect for a student budget.

Now, with the abundance of online food content, pita bread is everywhere. The desire to recreate it at home, to truly experience the difference between store-bought and homemade, finally became overwhelming. I took the plunge, and the results were astonishing. The homemade pita bread far surpassed my expectations; they were so incredibly fresh and flavorful that I was instantly hooked. Baking a batch of warm, fragrant pitas is now a cherished kitchen ritual.

Its simple ingredients and straightforward cooking process make pita incredibly convenient. I can easily store a batch for up to a week, ready to be used whenever I need them. The real magic lies in its adaptability. These pockets are a blank canvas for culinary creativity. A quick smear of peanut butter makes a satisfying snack on a busy weeknight. When time allows, I can transform them into something truly special. The soft, pliable texture is perfect for little hands, too. My daughter adores them, happily holding them herself and dipping them into her favorite sauces. It's a meal that satisfies everyone, from the simplest to the most sophisticated palates. This flatbread isn't just a convenient food; it's a foundation for countless meals, a way to explore different flavors, and a source of joy for my family.

This cookbook celebrates the flexibility and deliciousness of leavened flatbreads, showcasing some of my absolute favorites: Pide, Cauliflower Flatbread, and Lentil Pita Pocket. What's truly wonderful is that these breads all stem from one simple, foundational recipe.

Pide, in particular, are especially popular in my household. They've become our go-to pizza alternative, a weekly tradition we look forward to every Saturday. There's something incredibly satisfying about creating these warm, flavorful breads from scratch, topping them with our favorite ingredients, and sharing them with family and friends.

Flatbread / Pita

THE ART OF BAKING: THE UNIVERSAL LANGUAGE OF BREAD

Perfect for scooping up curries, soups, or dips, these warm and fluffy breads are a delicious addition to any meal. Try making a chimichurri tofu flatbread sandwich for an exciting twist.

INGREDIENTS

4 cups (650 g) bread flour
2 teaspoons sea salt
3 tablespoons olive oil, more to drizzle
340 mL (1½ cups) room temperature water
1 teaspoon oil to drizzle on dough
¼ cup semolina or bread flour for dusting

Yeast preparation
1 teaspoon active yeast
1 teaspoon maple syrup
¼ cup warm water (about 100°F)

TIPS

- *NO BUBBLES? NO PROBLEM! If the yeast mixture doesn't foam after 10 minutes, it's inactive. Start over with fresh yeast.*
- *HANDS-ON FLATBREADS: For a more rustic touch, stretch the flatbreads by hand (rolling pin optional). When rolling your flatbread, if you see a lot of bubbles, be careful not to press too hard and break them. Roll the bread lightly.*
- *SMART PITA TIMING: You can divide the dough in half and make flatbread and pita at the same time. Let the pita bread rise while the oven preheats for the flatbreads.*

Activate the Yeast: Combine yeast, maple syrup, and warm water, and let it foam for 10 minutes.

Make the Dough: In a large mixing bowl, whisk together the flour and salt. Create a well in the center and pour in the oil. Combine the activated yeast mixture with the remaining water and add it to the bowl. Using a dough whisk or your hands, mix all the ingredients together until a shaggy dough forms.

Knead the Dough: Turn the dough out onto a lightly floured surface and knead for 5–7 minutes to achieve a smooth and elastic dough that's not sticky.

Let the Dough Rise: Lightly grease a large bowl. Place the dough inside, turning it to coat with oil. Cover the bowl with a tea towel and let the dough rise in a warm place for about 2 hours or until doubled in size. I typically proof my dough in the oven.

Preheat the Oven: Place the dough bowl on your kitchen counter and preheat your oven to 450°F (232°C).

Flatbreads: Divide the dough into four equal pieces. On a lightly floured surface, gently roll each piece into a circle about 8–10 inches in diameter and ¼ inch thick. You can also use your hands to stretch the dough into a round shape.

Lightly sprinkle baking sheet with semolina flour. Place the rolled-out flatbreads on the baking sheet, leaving about an inch of space between them and bake for about 5 minutes or until golden brown and slightly puffed. Remove from the oven and cool on a wire rack.

Pita: Divide the dough into eight equal pieces (about 150 g each). Lightly dust a baking sheet with semolina flour. Shape each dough piece into a ball by stretching the sides and tucking them underneath. Gently flatten the ball with your palm on a lightly floured surface. Use a rolling pin to roll it out into a ¼-inch-thick, 5-inch round.

Place the rolled-out pita bread on the prepared baking sheet, bottom side up, leaving about an inch of space between them. Repeat with the remaining dough. Cover with a kitchen towel and let rest for 15 minutes. Bake for 8–10 minutes or until golden brown and puffed. A pocket may form in the middle as it bakes. Remove from the oven and cool on a wire rack. Enjoy warm!

Cauliflower Flatbread

VEGGIE POWER: GOLDEN & CRISPY

Make it a family affair! Serve these flatbreads with a refreshing salad or crispy okra fries.

Flatbread (page 96)
1 cup (250 g) cauliflower florets
½ teaspoon cumin powder
¼ teaspoon sea salt
1 tablespoon olive oil and more to drizzle
¼ cup onion, thinly sliced
½ cup yellow bell pepper, thinly sliced
Handful of fresh cilantro, chopped

Sauce
Mango Chutney (page 28)
Tamarind Sauce (page 34)

These soft and chewy flatbreads, cooked on the griddle or in the oven, are topped with an irresistible mix of roasted cauliflower, onions, peppers, and fresh cilantro, then drizzled with a tangy homemade sauce for a flavor fiesta.

Roast the Cauliflower: Heat a pan over medium heat and add oil. Add the cauliflower florets and sauté for 1 minute. Season with salt and cumin powder. Cover the pan and cook for 3 minutes. Uncover, stir, and cook for an additional 5–6 minutes or until golden brown.

Cook the Flatbread: Prepare the flatbread dough as directed in the book. For convenience, store-bought flatbread can be substituted.

Preheat a griddle over medium–high heat. Drizzle a teaspoon of oil onto the griddle. Gently place the flatbread dough on the hot surface. Cook for 2 minutes per side or until golden brown. Use a slotted spatula to press down on the flatbread while cooking, similar to making aaloo paratha.

Make the Sauce: To make the tangy sauce, combine mango chutney and tamarind paste. Start with a small amount and add more to taste. Alternatively, choose another sauce from this book.

Assemble and Enjoy: Spread the mango-tamarind sauce evenly over the cooked flatbread. Then, layer on the roasted cauliflower, chopped onion, bell pepper, and fresh cilantro. Enjoy fresh!

TIPS

- *VEGGIE VERSATILITY: Swap the cauliflower with seasonal favorites like okra, potato, beans, or cabbage!*
- *HANDHELD DELIGHT: Cut the flatbread in half and fold for a portable sandwich.*
- *BAKED GOODNESS: Instead of topping the cooked flatbread, you can bake the flatbread dough with the sauce and roasted cauliflower already on it. Bake until golden brown (about 10 minutes), then drizzle with homemade Caesar dressing.*

Pide / Turkish Pizza

SAVORY TWIST: PIZZA'S ANATOLIAN COUSIN

I suggest a buffet of pide with a variety of exotic sauces, accompanied by a Tempeh Caesar salad. Let everyone create their own pide and share for a memorable night.

INGREDIENTS

Flatbread (page 96)
1 tablespoon rosemary (optional)
¼ cup semolina flour for dusting
1 tablespoon olive oil for brushing
Handful of dill
Handful of black sesame seeds
Handful of nigella seeds (optional)

Sauce
Eggplant and Pepper Dip (page 42)
Cashew Cream Cloud Dip (page 48)

Pide, a Turkish pizza packed with flavor and endless possibilities, is about to become your new go-to recipe! This recipe uses a simple flatbread dough that transforms into delicious boat-shaped pockets filled with your favorite toppings.

Prepare the Dough: Follow my flatbread recipe and let the dough rise for 2 hours until it doubles. Slightly punch down the dough, then divide it into four equal pieces.

Shape the Boats: Lightly dust a surface with semolina flour. Gently roll each dough piece into a 10–12-inches long oval, and 5–6-inches wide. Alternatively, use floured hands to stretch it into a boat shape. Leave a 1-inch border on the sides and a 2-inch border on the top and bottom for folding.

Get Creative with Fillings: Here are some delicious filling ideas, but feel free to experiment!

Eggplant and pepper dip, jerk tofu, cilantro pesto, chimichurri, peanut sauce, tamarind sauce, mango chutney, lachha paratha wrap potato mix, tempeh masala dosa mix, grilled mushrooms, and even pineapple.

Assemble Your Pide: Spread your chosen sauce and filling in the center of the dough. Brush the edges with water. Fold the sides of the dough inward over the filling, creating a boat shape. Fold the top and bottom ends inward to close the boat. Pinch the side edges to seal. Brush the sides with olive oil and sprinkle with sesame or nigella seeds.

Bake to Perfection: Preheat your oven to 450°F. For even baking, I use a perforated pizza tray and bake two pides at a time for 12–15 minutes, or until golden brown.

Serve & Enjoy: Let the pide cool slightly on a cutting board. Slice, garnish with fresh herbs, and savor the deliciousness!

TIPS

- *TEMPERATURE MATTERS: Aim for room temperature (around 70°F) for rising dough. I like to put the dough bowl inside the oven to proof.*
- *ROSEMARY, A LITTLE MAGIC IN EVERY BITE: Want the most aromatic pide? Just swirl a tablespoon of rosemary into the dough. It's pure magic.*
- *ENDLESS OPTIONS: Get creative with fillings and toppings to personalize your pide! Mango Chutney pide is a must-try!*
- *STORAGE: Enjoy your pide warm or cold, it's delicious either way!*

Lentil Pita Pocket

LOVE AT FIRST BITE: WRAPPED IN DELICIOUSNESS

These lentil pitas, served with roasted vegetables and mango sparkling soda, are a great choice for your next outdoor gathering.

INGREDIENTS

For Lentil Balls

½ cup split chickpeas (chana dal), dried
½ cup split black lentils (urad dal), dried
½ cup yellow mung beans, dried
4 cups water for soaking lentils
¾ cup water for blending lentil
1 tablespoon (20 g) ginger, chopped
1½ teaspoons salt
1 teaspoon cumin powder
1 cup dill, roughly chopped
1 tablespoon roasted sesame seed
2 cups olive oil for frying

For Salad

Handful of mixed greens
A few green onions, finely chopped
Handful of cilantro, finely chopped
1 bell pepper, diced
1 tomato, diced
1 lemon

Sauce

Sunshine Yogurt Dip (page 38)

TIPS

- *MULTITASKING: While the lentil balls cook, efficiently use your time by preparing the salad and warming the pita bread.*
- *WATER BALANCE: Gradually add water to the lentil mixture until it reaches a consistency that allows you to comfortably form balls. If the mixture is too thick, add a few tablespoons of water. If it's too thin or runny, add a few tablespoons of rice flour or all-purpose flour.*

Prepare the Lentils: Mix the lentils in a big bowl and rinse a few times. Soak them in 4 cups of water overnight.

Make the Lentil Mixture: Drain the soaked lentils using a strainer. Add the lentils to a blender or food processor along with ginger, salt, cumin powder, and dill. Blend for 30–40 seconds. Slowly add water while blending until you have a thick mixture. You can make the mix smooth or leave it slightly chunky. Transfer the mixture to a bowl. Stir in roasted sesame seeds. Cover the bowl and let the mixture marinate for 30 minutes.

Fry the Lentil Balls: Heat oil in a deep pan over medium heat. To test the oil temperature, drop a small piece of lentil mixture into the oil. If it rises slowly to the surface, the oil is hot enough; if it rises quickly, reduce the heat.

Scoop out 1 tablespoon of the mixture and shape it into a ball using your hands (or a spoon). Gently add the lentil balls to the hot oil. Fry them for 10 minutes over medium heat, then increase the heat to medium-high for a few minutes to achieve a golden brown color. Reduce the heat to medium-low and quickly remove the cooked lentil balls with a skimmer, placing them on a plate lined with paper towels to drain excess oil. Repeat with the remaining lentil mixture.

Prepare the Salad: Combine salad mix with a pinch of salt and a squeeze of lemon juice in a bowl.

Assemble and Enjoy: Warm pita. Fill each pita with salad, lentil balls, and your desired amount of herb yogurt sauce.

Khobz / Burger Bun

BIG, BOLD, & BEAUTIFUL: THE BURGER ADVENTURE STARTS HERE

Khobz is a delightful flatbread that's both soft and dense, making it a perfect accompaniment to soups, salads, or sandwiches.

INGREDIENTS

3½ cups (560 g) bread flour
½ cup (80 g) semolina flour
¼ cup semolina flour for dusting
2 teaspoons sea salt
300 mL (1¼ cups) room-temperature water
1 tablespoon olive oil to brush on bun
1 tablespoon black sesame seeds

Yeast preparation
1 teaspoon active dry yeast
1 teaspoon maple syrup
¼ cup warm water

TIPS

- *DOUGH ADJUSTMENT: Fine-tune flour or water based on your climate's humidity.*
- *STORAGE: Store leftover khobz in an airtight container to maintain freshness. They will stay fresh for 3–4 days.*
- *CAST-IRON PAN: I use my cast-iron pan to create steam inside the oven. Whenever I am done with khobz, I take the pan out and bake the buns.*

Proof the Yeast: Combine yeast, maple syrup, and warm water in a cup. Let it sit for 10 minutes until foamy. This activates the yeast.

Mix the Dough: In a large bowl, whisk together flour and salt. Add the yeast mixture and water. Combine well, cover the bowl with a cotton cloth, and let the dough rest for 10 minutes.

Knead the Dough: Transfer the dough to a lightly floured surface. Knead for 5–10 minutes until smooth and elastic. Add more flour if sticky, or water if dry. The dough should be slightly tacky but not stick to your hands.

First Rise: Place the dough in a bowl lightly dusted with semolina flour. Cover with a cotton cloth and let it rise in a warm place for 40 minutes.

For Khobz: Divide the dough into two equal pieces (about 500 g each). Take one of these pieces and cut it in half again. Gently stretch and tuck the sides of each piece to form a smooth, round ball. On a lightly floured surface dusted with semolina flour, use the palms of your hands to flatten the balls into 5–6-inch circle that are about 1 inch thick. Transfer the circle dough to a baking pan that has been lightly dusted with semolina flour. Sprinkle the tops of the dough with semolina flour, cover them with a tea towel, and let them rise for another 30 minutes.

Preheat the Oven: Preheat your oven to 450°F (232°C). Place a pan of water on the bottom rack to create steam for baking the khobz.

Score Khobz: Using a sharp knife or lame, score the top of each khobz with a design. Bake for 12–15 minutes or until golden brown and let it cool on a wire rack.

For Burger Buns: Divide the remaining dough into five equal pieces (about 100 g each). Shape them into balls and flatten slightly. Sprinkle sesame seeds on a surface and gently press the tops of the buns into them to create a sesame seed topping. Place them on a baking sheet dusted with semolina flour. Cover with a tea towel and let them rise for 30 minutes. Before baking, brush the tops of the buns with olive oil or coconut milk for a golden-brown finish. Bake for 8–10 minutes or until golden brown. I usually bake the khobz first, then the buns. Remove from the oven and let cool on a wire rack. Enjoy fresh!

The Quest for the Perfect Veggie Burger

Growing up in Nepal, beans were a staple in our kitchen. We savored a vast array of legumes, from black-eyed peas to fava beans. Each one offered a unique texture and flavor, but red kidney beans held a special place in my heart. I still cherish the memory of creamy red kidney bean soup, a dish that nourished my body and soul. These same beans found their way into my first cookbook, *Plant-Based Himalaya*, in the form of a hearty Rajma curry.

Nepal's culinary tradition revolves around plant-based delights. Burgers, however, were a new discovery after moving to America. While I enjoyed chicken burgers, my transition to a fully plant-based lifestyle in 2016 posed a challenge. Many veggie burgers on the market were loaded with additives and lacked the taste and texture I craved. Determined to create a healthy and satisfying alternative, I set off on an odyssey of experimentation, mixing various vegetables and grains. This recipe for kidney bean and quinoa burgers is the result of a delicious recipe development. Visually stunning and packed with protein and fiber, these burgers might just surprise you with their "better than beef" flavor (as my burger-loving father-in-law declared after his first bite!). Their versatility extends beyond burgers—I make large batches and freeze them for future use as pizza toppings or sandwich fillings. The possibilities are endless!

A Culinary Journey from Mother's Heart to Your Plate

Motherhood has instilled in me a deep desire to nourish my daughter with wholesome, homemade meals. Witnessing her delight at each bite reminds me of the importance of food traditions passed down through generations. I find inspiration in these moments of synchronicity, and that's how many of my recipes are created.

Seeking a bun that could stand up to the burger's juicy weight, I looked beyond traditional burger buns. My culinary explorations led to the bustling streets of Morocco, where the slightly chewy texture of Khobz bread offered the perfect inspiration. For the fillings, I turned to another global favorite—eggplant. This versatile vegetable outshine cultural boundaries. The Fried Eggplant Burger recipe embodies rich kaleidescope of flavors. From Nepali eggplant curries to fried eggplant dips, its potential is limitless. While researching for this cookbook, I discovered the beautiful overlap between Nepali and Mediterranean Blue Zone diets, both of which emphasize the use of fresh produce and fragrant spices.

So, take a bite—and join me on a taste adventure around the globe, all from your kitchen! These burgers are your passport to a world of flavor, a delicious journey inspired by my travels and the vibrant cuisines I've encountered.

Kidney Bean & Quinoa Burger

SUPERFOOD SENSATION: A WHOLESOME & DELICIOUS PATTY

You have to try this: a hearty kidney bean and quinoa burger, crispy, spicy timur fries, and a refreshing lemon soda. It's seriously the best burger combo ever!

INGREDIENTS

2 cups red kidney beans
¾ cup red quinoa
2 ears corn in the cob
1½ cup red onion, finely diced
½ teaspoon turmeric
2 teaspoons sumac powder
2 teaspoons cumin powder
1 tablespoon garlic, minced
1 tablespoon ginger, minced
1 cup cilantro, chopped
6 whole green chilies, finely chopped
1 cup chickpea flour
1½ teaspoons sea salt
1 cup olive oil

<u>To assemble burger</u>
Burger Buns (page 104)
Handful of spinach
A few dill pickles
1 or 2 red tomatoes, sliced
A few red onion rings

<u>Sauce</u>
Guacamole (page 44)

TIPS

- *ELEVATE YOUR MEAL: Pair your burgers with homemade buns and timur fries.*
- *GET CREATIVE: Explore the sauces in this cookbook to create your perfect burger. The versatile bean mix can also be enjoyed as a vibrant salad.*
- *FREEZE AND STORE: For longer storage, line a baking sheet with parchment paper, arrange the patties in a single layer, and freeze them until solid (about 2 hours). Then, transfer the frozen patties to a airtight container and store them in the freezer for future use.*

These unforgettable kidney bean and quinoa burgers combine a satisfying crunch with a juicy center, all while being packed with protein and nutrients.

Prep the Beans: Rinse the kidney beans and soak them in 4 cups of water for at least 8 hours, or preferably overnight. Transfer the soaked beans with all the soaking water to an Instant Pot with a pinch of salt and cook on high pressure for 6 minutes. Let pressure release naturally for 20 minutes, then carefully release any remaining pressure. Drain the beans in a strainer and let them cool. For a quicker option, use canned beans.

Cook the Quinoa: Bring 2 cups of water to a rolling boil in a saucepan. Rinse the quinoa once under running water. Add quinoa to the boiling water and reduce heat to low. Cover the pan, and simmer for 15–20 minutes, or until all the liquid is absorbed. Remove from heat, fluff with a fork, and let it cool.

Boil the Corn: Bring another pot of water to a boil. Add the corn and cook for 4 minutes. Drain the water, let the corn cool slightly, and then cut the kernels from the cob. Alternatively, you can substitute 1 cup of canned corn.

Combine the Ingredients: In a large mixing bowl, combine the cooked kidney beans, boiled quinoa, corn, onion, turmeric, sumac powder, cumin powder, ginger, garlic, cilantro, green chilies, and salt.

Marinate the Patties: Using your hands, massage the mixture well, combining all ingredients. I like to keep the beans a little chunky. Gradually add chickpea flour until the mixture holds its shape. Cover the bowl with a plate and let it marinate for 30 minutes.

Make the Patties: Using your hands, gently shape the mixture into patties of your desired size. Place the patties on a plate lightly dusted with chickpea flour to prevent sticking. I usually make 20 patties and freeze half of them for later.

Cook the Patties: Heat 2 tablespoons of oil in a large skillet over medium heat. Carefully add 2–3 patties to the hot oil, leaving space between them. Cook for 3 minutes per side, or until the patties are golden brown and cooked through.

Assemble and Enjoy: Lightly toast burger buns. Spread the bottom bun with guacamole, then layer with fresh spinach leaves, the cooked patty, pickle slices, juicy tomato slices, and thinly sliced onion. Top with the other bun and enjoy!

Fried Eggplant Burger

MEATLESS MASTERPIECE: BITE INTO BLISS

Prepare to be amazed by the juiciest fried eggplant burger you've ever tasted. Combined with creamy avocado and potato salad, it's a meal that will redefine your burger expectations.

INGREDIENTS

2 medium eggplants
½ cup corn flour
¼ cup rice flour
1 teaspoon oregano, dried
1 teaspoon garlic powder
2 green chilies, finely chopped
1½ teaspoons sea salt
½ teaspoon turmeric
2 cups water for batter
2 cups oil to fry

To assemble burger
Burger Buns (page 104)
1 cup mixed greens
½ cup red onions, sliced
2 medium tomatoes, sliced

Sauce
Spicy Timur Sauce (page 32)
Mint Chutney (page 40)

TIPS

- *FRY WISELY: To maintain oil temperature for crispy eggplant, don't crowd the pan. If the oil is too hot, turn the heat to medium–low.*
- *FLAVOR ADVENTURE: Experiment with spices and herbs in the batter. For a faster and equally tasty meal, marinate the eggplant slices in salt and turmeric for 30 minutes, then pan-fry until golden brown. The resulting eggplant is incredibly soft, juicy, and perfect with rice and dal.*

Prep the Eggplant: Wash the eggplants and trim off the tops. Slice the eggplants crosswise into ¼-inch-thick rounds. In a large bowl, combine water and ½ teaspoon of salt. Add the eggplant slices and let them soak for 30 minutes to draw out any bitterness.

Make the Batter: In a large bowl, combine the flour, dried oregano, garlic powder, finely chopped green chili, turmeric, the remaining salt (1 teaspoon) and water to form a batter.

Fry the Eggplant: Heat oil in a deep pan over medium heat (around 350°F). Coat eggplant slices evenly in batter, then carefully add to the hot oil. Fry until golden brown and crispy, about 2–3 minutes per side. Transfer to a paper towel-lined plate to drain. For a less oily version, pan-fry the coated eggplant in a few tablespoons of oil.

Assemble and Enjoy: Toast the buns. Layer with crisp lettuce, juicy tomato, sliced onion, fragrant mint chutney, spicy timur sauce, and crispy fried eggplant. Enjoy!

Baguette / Homemade Bread

SKIP THE STORE: BAKE MORE AT HOME

Toast your homemade baguettes and enjoy a taste of France. Or, make amazing sandwiches with fresh veggies, grilled tofu, and your favorite sauce from this book.

INGREDIENTS

4½ cups (700 g) bread flour
¼ cup extra bread flour for dusting
2 teaspoons salt
455 mL (1¾ cups + 2 tablespoons) room temperature water
1 teaspoon active dry yeast

TIPS

- *LARGER BAGUETTES: Divide dough into three pieces for bigger loaves. Bake two to three baguettes per baking sheet, ensuring they have ample space to rise and expand during baking.*
- *SCORING: Using a sharp knife or baker's lame, make three or four diagonal slashes across the dough's surface. Each slash should be about 1/2 inch deep.*
- *SHAPING BAGUETTE: Shaping the baguettes into pointed ends may take practice, but even if they're not perfect, your bread will still be delicious.*
- *VERSATILE YIELD: This recipe makes three perfect sandwich baguettes and two bonus small loaves.*

While not a traditional baguette, this easy, no-fuss bread is a perfect choice for a quick and satisfying meal.

Make the Dough: In a large mixing bowl, combine the flour, salt, and yeast. Gradually add water, mixing with a wooden spatula or your hand until a rough, shaggy dough forms. Knead for 1 minute, until a ball forms. This dough will be somewhat sticky. Cover the bowl with a damp tea towel and let it rise in a warm place for 2 hours until it doubles in size (I proof mine in the oven and set a timer).

Knead and Rest: Turn the dough out onto a lightly floured surface, using floured hands to prevent sticking. Knead for 5 minutes, using the stretch and fold method until the dough is smooth, elastic, and no longer sticky. It should feel supple and springy. Place the kneaded dough back in the bowl, cover with the damp tea towel, and let it rise in a warm place for 2 more hours. For a richer flavor, refrigerate the covered dough overnight (12–14 hours).

Shape the Baguettes: Prepare a baker's couche by lightly flouring a clean tea towel or light cotton cloth. Generously flour a clean work surface. Divide the dough into four equal pieces. Gently stretch each piece into a 4 x 6-inch rectangle. Fold the bottom half lengthwise, then fold the top half toward you to create a seam. Gently press along the seam with your palm to seal.

Roll the Baguettes: On a lightly floured surface, and using lightly floured hands, gently roll each piece of dough outward from the center, stretching and shaping it into a long, tapered baguette with pointed ends. Carefully transfer each shaped baguette to the prepared couche, leaving about an inch of space between them to allow for expansion during proofing. Lightly dust the tops of the baguettes with flour to prevent them from drying out. Cover the couche with a dry clean cotton cloth and let the baguettes proof for 30–45 minutes.

Preheat the Oven: Preheat your oven to 475°F (245°C). Place a pan of water on the bottom rack to create steam during baking. Lightly flour a baking sheet. Gently transfer the baguettes to the baking sheet, spacing them about 1.5 inches apart. Score the tops diagonally with a sharp knife (or lame) to allow for even expansion.

Bake to Golden Brown: Bake for 8 minutes, then carefully turn the baguettes for even browning. Bake for another 8 minutes or until golden brown. Remove the baguettes from the oven and let them cool on a wire rack and serve warm.

Falafelball Sub

FLAVOR BOMB: A MEDITERRANEAN DELIGHT

Falafel gets a delicious upgrade with a classic Syrian biwaz salad and a zesty Italian-Nepali fusion marinara sauce. Pair your falafel sub with vibrant bitter gourd pickle salad for a complete meal.

INGREDIENTS

2 cups dry black chickpeas (chana)
4 cups water for soaking
1 tablespoon garlic, minced
1 tablespoon ginger, minced
2 small habaneros, finely chopped
1 teaspoon whole allspice pepper
1 teaspoon nutmeg powder
2-inch long cinnamon stick
6 pods cardamom
1 teaspoon cumin seeds
1 teaspoon coriander seeds
10 cloves
1 anise
¼ cup olive oil
1 bunch cilantro, finely chopped
2 teaspoons sea salt
17 oz (480 g) extra firm tofu, crumbled
1½ cups red onions, finely chopped
¼ cup chickpea flour (besan)
3 tablespoons toasted sesame seeds
Biwaz for garnish (page 56)
4 hoagie buns (page 112)

Sauce
2 cups marinara (page 26)

TIPS

- *MARINARA PREFERENCE: Adjust the amount of marinara sauce to your liking. The falafel will absorb some of the sauce, so you may need to add a little extra water to thin it out.*
- *BUN CHOICE: Opt for a hoagie bun that's not overly soft for a sturdier sandwich.*
- *STORAGE: This recipe yields about seventy-five falafel balls. Use as needed and freeze the rest for up to three months.*

Cook the Chickpeas: Wash and soak the chickpeas in 4 cups of water overnight. Cook them with 1 teaspoon of salt in an Instant Pot for 6 minutes on high pressure. Alternatively, boil them in a pot until tender (about 30 minutes). Drain the cooked chickpeas, reserving ½ cup of the cooking water.

Make the Falafel Base: In a food processor, pulse the cooked chickpeas with ½ cup of reserved cooking water for about 20 seconds, until they are coarsely ground. You want a chunky texture, not a completely smooth paste. If the mixture is too dry add more water, a tablespoon at a time. Transfer the coarsely ground chickpeas to a large bowl.

Prepare the Spices: Heat a pan over medium heat. Add allspice pepper, cinnamon stick, cardamom, anise, cumin seeds, coriander seeds, and cloves. Dry-roast the spices for a few minutes until fragrant, stirring frequently. Let them cool slightly. In a mortar and pestle or spice blender, blend the spices.

Combine the Falafel Mixture: Add the ground spices, nutmeg powder, crumbled tofu, gram flour, onion, remaining salt, habanero, oil, sesame seeds, and chopped cilantro to the bowl with the chickpea mixture. Gently combine, keeping the tofu in small chunks. Cover the bowl and refrigerate the falafel mixture for at least an hour (or up to two hours for best flavor).

Bake the Falafel Balls: Preheat oven to 400°F (200°C). Line a baking sheet with parchment paper. Take about 1 tablespoon of the falafel mixture and roll it into a ball between your palms to form smooth, round balls. Arrange the balls in rows on the prepared baking sheet. Bake the falafel balls for 40 minutes, flipping them over halfway through baking. Take the falafel balls out and let them cool.

Assemble and Enjoy: Gently warm the marinara sauce in a saucepan over low heat. Add the falafel balls and simmer for 10 minutes to allow the flavors to soak in. Toast or warm the hoagie buns to your preference. Liberally fill the bottom bun with biwaz salad, top with warm falafel balls and a generous spoonful of marinara sauce. Finish with a final layer of biwaz salad for a fresh and flavorful garnish. Enjoy!

Grilled Mushroom Sandwich

SMOKY & SAVORY: PLANT-BASED PERFECTION

For a truly satisfying feast, complement your grilled mushroom sandwich with the delightful crunch of okra fries or the flavorful jackfruit empanadas.

INGREDIENTS

8 oz (226 g) oyster mushrooms
½ cup onion, chopped
2 cloves garlic
1 teaspoon whole allspice pepper
1 serrano pepper, chopped
2 teaspoons pomegranate molasses
½ teaspoon salt
1 bunch lettuce, washed and dried
½ cup cilantro, chopped
2 tablespoons olive oil
1 baguette (page 112)

Sauce (optional)
Caesar Dressing (page 30)
Spicy Timur Sauce (page 32)

TIPS

- *PICK THE PERFECT MUSHROOMS: Use large, fresh oyster mushrooms for the best texture.*
- *STORAGE: Repurpose leftover marinated mushrooms in salads or wraps.*
- *AIOLI SAUCE: For a truly exceptional aioli, use a good-quality, extra-virgin olive oil. Crush several garlic cloves into a fine paste using a mortar and pestle. Slowly drizzle in 3–4 tablespoons of the olive oil, a teaspoon at a time, while continuously emulsifying the mixture with a steady, circular motion of the pestle. This process requires patience, but the result is worth it. As the aioli thickens, season with salt to taste. Once the desired consistency is reached, transfer the aioli to a serving container and use as desired.*

Discover the magic of marinated oyster mushrooms—the perfect filling for your next sandwich.

Prep the Mushrooms: Gently wash any dirt off the oyster mushrooms. Trim and discard the tough stem ends. Thinly slice the larger caps (or slice thicker for a chewier texture).

Make the Marinade: Combine chopped onion, garlic, serrano pepper, allspice pepper, pomegranate molasses, and salt in a blender. Blend until smooth. Taste and adjust the amount of serrano pepper for your desired level of spiciness.

Marinate the Mushrooms: In a bowl, gently toss the sliced oyster mushrooms with the prepared marinade, ensuring all the mushrooms are coated. Cover the bowl tightly and refrigerate for 30 minutes to an hour, to allow the flavors to fully develop.

Heat the Griddle: Preheat a griddle or large skillet over high heat. Add oil to coat the pan.

Grill the Mushrooms: Arrange the marinated mushrooms in a single layer on the hot griddle, ensuring they aren't overcrowded. Cook for 6–10 minutes, flipping them occasionally with tongs or a spatula, until they are golden brown, tender, and slightly caramelized.

Assemble and Enjoy: On a fresh, warm baguette, build your sandwich by layering crisp lettuce, juicy tomato slices, and the savory grilled mushrooms. Drizzle generously with Caesar dressing for extra flavor and richness. Garnish with a sprinkle of chopped fresh cilantro for a touch of freshness. Enjoy immediately!

Hummus Sandwich

HAPPINESS BETWEEN SLICES: NOURISHING VEGGIE POWER

The richness of the sandwich is beautifully balanced by the bright, refreshing flavors of a freshly squeezed lemon sparkling soda or a subtly tangy kombucha.

INGREDIENTS

A few sourdough slices
1 medium cucumber, thinly sliced
½ red bell pepper, thinly sliced
½ cup purple cabbage, thinly sliced
A few yellow cherry tomatoes, cut in half
½ cup arugula
¼ cup red onion, thinly sliced
Salt and black pepper for taste
Half lemon, to drizzle on top
½ cup Pumpkin Hummus (page 46)
1 teaspoon toasted black sesame seeds

This decadent open-faced sandwich is bursting with fresh flavors and textures. Creamy hummus serves as the base, while a colorful medley of vegetables adds a delightful crunch. Toasted sourdough offers a sturdy platform for this flavor fiesta, making it perfect for an appetizing lunch or a light and refreshing brunch.

Prep the Vegetables: Wash and chop all the vegetables. In a large bowl, toss the prepared vegetables with a pinch of salt, freshly ground black pepper, and a squeeze of fresh lemon juice. Add a dollop of hummus and combine well, ensuring all the vegetables are lightly coated.

Toast the Bread: Heat a pan or griddle over medium heat. Add a drizzle of olive oil or a pat of vegan butter. Toast the sourdough slices until golden brown and crisp on both sides.

Assemble the Sandwich and Enjoy: Spread a generous layer of hummus salad on each toasted bread slice. Squeeze some fresh lemon juice over the sandwich, and sprinkle with toasted black sesame seeds for a nutty flavor. For an extra layer of flavor, drizzle with mint chutney, if desired.

TIPS

- *HUMMUS OPTIONS: Homemade hummus is fantastic, but store-bought varieties offer a convenient alternative. Choose a flavor that complements the other ingredients. Consider roasted red pepper hummus, or roasted garlic hummus.*
- *STORAGE: Store leftover hummus in an airtight container in the refrigerator for up to a week. Enjoy it on crackers, as a veggie dip, or in wraps for a quick and healthy lunch.*

Welcome to *Garden Exotica's* Savory Symphony! Discover a world of plant-based flavors and textures, perfect for everything from quick weeknight meals to potluck feasts. Enjoy the journey of creating delicious, wholesome dishes for yourself and your loved ones. Experiment with different sauces to unlock a universe of fusion flavors.

SAVORY

Pinto Bean & Rice With Jerk Tofu

CARIBBEAN COMFORT: AN ISLAND FEAST

The bold flavors of the jerk tofu and pinto bean and rice are beautifully balanced by a creamy northern white bean soup, adding warmth and depth to your dining experience.

INGREDIENTS

1 cup basmati rice
1 cup pinto beans, dried
4 cups water
2 tablespoons olive oil
1 teaspoon cumin seeds
½ teaspoon turmeric
1 teaspoon salt
½ teaspoon lemon zest
Handful of mixed greens for garnish

Marinate Tofu
Jerk Sauce (page 36)
14 oz (396 g) extra firm tofu
4 tablespoons olive oil for frying

TIPS

- *JERK TOFU REIMAGINED: Jerk-marinated tofu is a delicious and versatile ingredient! Enjoy it in sandwiches, burgers, wraps, and salads or as a flavorful side dish. Get creative and invent your own fusion recipes.*
- *STORAGE: Store leftovers in an airtight container in the fridge for up to 24 hours. Reheat gently on the stovetop.*
- *RICE VARIATION: Pokhreli rice, with its delightful aroma, would be my first choice if I could find it here in the US. For a fun variation, experiment with different rice varieties.*

Soak the Pinto Beans: Rinse the dried pinto beans thoroughly. Soak them in 2 cups of water for at least 4 hour or overnight.

Marinate the Tofu: Wash and pat the tofu dry with a clean kitchen towel. Cut the tofu into bite-sized cubes and place them in a bowl. Pour the jerk sauce over the tofu cubes and toss to coat them evenly. Let the tofu marinate for at least 1 hour or even overnight in the refrigerator for deeper flavor.

Soak the Rice: Wash the basmati rice in cold water at least four times. Swirl the grains and drain the water each time, until the water runs clear. Soak the rinsed rice in 2 cups of fresh water for 30 minutes.

Cook the Pinto Beans: Heat a pan over medium–high heat. Add oil and temper cumin seeds. Once the cumin seeds sizzle, drain the soaked pinto beans and add them to the pan. Season with turmeric powder and salt. Stir well and sauté for 2–3 minutes. Reduce heat to medium–low, cover the pan with a lid, and cook the beans for 10 minutes or until tender. Stir occasionally.

Cook the Rice: Add the pre-soaked rice (with the water it soaked in) and lemon zest to the pan containing the cooked pinto beans. Stir well to combine all the ingredients. Increase the heat to medium. Bring the mixture to a boil, then reduce the heat to medium–low. Cover the pan with a lid. Cook for 15 minutes or until the rice is fluffy and all the liquid is absorbed. Once cooked, turn off the heat and let the rice steam, covered, for an additional 5 minutes to ensure it's perfectly fluffy.

Cook the Jerk Tofu: While the rice is cooking, heat another pan over medium heat. Add 2 tablespoons of oil. Once hot, add half of the marinated tofu cubes. Cook for 2–3 minutes per side or until golden brown and crispy. You can drizzle some extra jerk sauce over the tofu while cooking for added flavor and moisture. Repeat the process with the remaining tofu cubes.

Assemble and Serve: For a fresh element, add a bed of mixed greens to two serving plates. Divide the cooked rice and pinto beans between the plates, top with jerk tofu and any remaining jerk sauce for an extra flavorful touch. Alternatively, serve the rice, beans, and tofu mixed together in a bowl with the jerk sauce on the side. Enjoy!

Rice: A Global Grain

Rice dishes are a global staple, enjoyed in countless variations from boiled rice and fried rice to porridge and gumbo. Nepal and India cultivate a wide array of rice varieties, each with unique characteristics in weight, size, and flavor, thanks to their diverse topographic regions. Archaeologists have traced rice cultivation back over eight thousand years in China, its influence spreading across Asia along ancient trade routes. Today, rice is a cornerstone food for over half the world's population, with each culture developing unique dishes and traditions around this humble grain. In Japan, perfectly cooked rice is considered an art form, served alongside meticulously prepared fish and vegetables in a kaiseki meal. In Southeast Asia, fragrant jasmine rice accompanies spicy curries in Thailand. And across the Indian subcontinent, aromatic basmati rice enhances rich dals and curries, while biryani, a layered rice dish with meat and vegetables, is a celebratory meal.

Rice's journey extends far beyond Asia. Jollof rice, a vibrant tomato-based dish, is a national treasure in West Africa. In the Caribbean, fragrant coconut rice is a staple alongside stews and jerk chicken. There are so many rice dishes from around the world I need to discover and create. This book shares my favorite rice dishes, inspired by my travels and everyday cooking.

Island Inspiration

Rice and beans are a backbone of Nepali cuisine, as well as many Asian and African diets. While I grew up familiar with various beans and legumes, pinto beans were a delightful discovery after moving to America. They've become a favorite in our household, thanks to their soft, creamy texture and versatility in rice dishes, soups, and salads.

This one-pot rice and beans recipe is a family favorite, thanks to its quick and easy preparation. Packed with protein and bursting with flavor, it creates minimal cleanup. Inspired by African-style rice and beans, Nepali pulao, and Indian biryani; its unique flavor comes from the bold spices of jerk sauce. These rich spices have also sparked my own culinary explorations, leading me to experiment with allspice pepper and nutmeg in a wider range of dishes.

Nepali Fried Rice

In Nepal, fried rice is a beloved afternoon treat. After a midday meal of dal (lentil soup) and bhat (rice), leftover rice is given a new life in a flavorful stir-fry with crisp carrots, tender cabbage, and sweet green peas. Fresh herbs and aromatic spices typically mingle with eggs or meat, and seasonal vegetables are always a welcome addition. This resourceful approach to using leftover rice is a common thread throughout Asian cuisines. Here I share another favorite rice dish that I cook very often—pineapple fried rice.

Pineapple & Dill Fried Rice

A FLAVORFUL FUSION: PARADISE IN A PAN

Tangy pineapple and fragrant dill infuse every grain of this delightful fried rice. A crisp side salad or creamy sunshine yogurt dip balances the sweet and savory flavors.

INGREDIENTS

1 cup basmati rice
1½ cups water for soaking
4 tablespoons coconut oil
1 cup pineapple, diced
1 teaspoon cumin seeds
½ teaspoon nigella seeds
2 dried red chilies, whole
1 teaspoon ginger, finely chopped
1 teaspoon garlic, finely chopped
2 fresh green chilies
1 small red onion, thinly sliced
¾ cup red bell peppers, thinly sliced
½ cup raw cashews
⅔ cup green beans, chopped diagonally
½ cup cabbage, shredded
½ cup carrot, shredded
½ teaspoon turmeric
1 teaspoon salt
¼ cup green onion, chopped
2 tablespoons fresh dill, chopped

TIPS

- *VEGGIE VERSATILITY: Feel free to customize with seasonal vegetables!*
- *PERFECT RICE: Precook the rice and let it cool completely before stir-frying. This prevents the rice from becoming mushy. Honestly, day-old leftover rice from a previous meal is my favorite and is probably the reason fried rice was invented.*

This Pineapple & Dill Fried Rice is a tropical twist on a classic. Combining sweet, tangy, and herbaceous flavors in every bite.

Cook the Rice: In a strainer, rinse the rice thoroughly under cold running water three to four times, swirling the grains and draining each time until the water runs clear. This removes excess starch for a fluffier texture. Combine the rinsed rice with water in a pot and let it soak for 15 to 30 minutes. Bring the water to a boil over medium–high heat. Reduce heat to medium–low, cover the pot, and simmer for 15 minutes or until the rice is cooked through and the water is absorbed. Remove from heat and let it cool completely on a flat plate while preparing the other ingredients.

Caramelize the Pineapple: Heat 1 tablespoon of coconut oil in a cast-iron skillet over medium heat. Add the chopped pineapple and cook, turning occasionally until golden brown and caramelized around the edges (about 5–7 minutes). Set aside on a plate.

Sauté the Vegetables: Heat the remaining coconut oil in a separate pan or wok over medium heat. Add cumin, nigella seeds, and dried red chilies. Temper them for a few seconds until fragrant. Stir in the chopped ginger, garlic, and green chilies. Sauté for a few seconds, then add the onion and bell peppers. Cook until the onion begins to soften, about 30 seconds. Add the cashews, green beans, and cabbage. Sauté for about a minute, stirring occasionally.

Simmer and Flavor: Stir in the turmeric powder and salt. Cover the pan and simmer for a few minutes or until the green beans are fully tender.

Assemble the Rice: Remove the lid and add the thinly sliced carrots, chopped fresh dill, cooked rice, and caramelized pineapple. Stir gently to combine all the ingredients without over mixing.

Serve and Enjoy: Transfer the pineapple and dill fried rice to a serving dish. Garnish with chopped green onions, fresh dill sprigs, and additional pineapple, if desired. Serve hot and enjoy!

Soya Chunks Étouffée

HEALTHY & HEARTY: COZY CAJUN FLAVORS

Serve your buttery étouffée over a bed of fluffy white rice, cornbread, or with a slice of soft homemade bread. The luscious sauce is so rich and flavorful, it will simply melt in your mouth.

INGREDIENTS

1 cup soya chunks
4 cups water
¼ cup olive oil
¼ cup all-purpose flour
3 cloves garlic, sliced
1 cup white onion, diced
1 cup red bell pepper, diced
2 stalks celery, chopped
½ teaspoon black pepper
¼ teaspoon red chili powder
1 teaspoon salt
2 medium tomatoes, diced
Handful of cilantro for garnish

TIPS

- *VERSATILE POWERHOUSE: Soya chunks are a nutritious and versatile ingredient, popular among vegetarians globally. They shine in curries, pickles, dumplings, pastas, and soups. While mild flavored on their own, they soak up spices beautifully, adding texture and depth.*
- *SIZE MATTERS: This recipe uses small soya chunks for faster cooking and better gravy absorption. If using larger chunks, chop them in half or quarters after soaking.*
- *TOASTED OR NOT? Soaking is a must, but for an extra layer of deliciousness, try frying the soaked soya chunks in 2–3 tablespoons of oil until they are beautifully golden brown and slightly crispy. This optional step adds a wonderful toasted flavor to the étouffée and any other dishes you create.*

Indulge in this delicious and satisfying meat-free étouffée, featuring tender soya chunks simmered in an umami-rich and savory roux. It's packed with protein and bursting with richness!

Soak the Soya Chunks: Rinse the dried soya chunks thoroughly under cold water. Cover them completely with 2 cups of cold water and let them soak for 10 minutes.

Prepare the Roux: Heat a heavy-bottomed dutch oven or cast-iron pan over medium heat. Add the oil and flour. Stir continuously using a whisk or wooden spoon. The mixture will begin to thicken and turn a light golden brown.

Cook the Roux: Reduce the heat to medium–low and continue stirring constantly for about 20 minutes. The roux should reach a dark brown color, resembling peanut butter.

Sauté the Vegetables: Add the garlic and cook for a few seconds until fragrant. Add the onion and cook for a few seconds more. Stir in the chopped bell pepper and celery. Sauté the vegetables over medium heat for 5 minutes or until softened.

Add Soya Chunks and Seasoning: Squeeze as much water possible from soya chunks and add to the pan. Cook for an additional 5 minutes and season with freshly grated black pepper, salt, and chili powder. Stir well to combine.

Simmer the Étouffée: Pour in the crushed or diced tomatoes. Combine well and cook for a minute. Add 2 cups of water and stir everything together. Bring to a simmer then cover the pot. Reduce heat to low and simmer for an additional 15–20 minutes or until the soya chunks are tender and the flavors have melded.

Serve and Enjoy: Once cooked through, your creamy and mouthwatering soya chunks étouffée is ready. Garnish with chopped fresh cilantro for an added touch of color and freshness. Enjoy!

Okra Fries

CRISPY & CRAVE-WORTHY: THE PERFECT SNACK

Serve these crunchy okra fries with your favorite dipping sauces like tamarind sauce, spicy timur sauce, or even mango chutney. They're a magnificent complement to any dish in this book.

INGREDIENTS

18 oz (510 g) okra
½ cup chickpea flour (besan)
2 teaspoons dried mango powder
1 teaspoon cumin powder
½ teaspoon red chili powder
1 teaspoon sea salt
1½ cups olive oil
½ teaspoon chaat masala

Sauce
Tamarind Sauce (page 34)

TIPS

- *ULTIMATE CRUNCH: The secret to perfectly crispy okra fries is thoroughly drying the okra before you slice it. Any excess moisture will cause the coating to steam rather than crisp up in the hot oil. I find that washing and drying the okra overnight works best.*
- *SELECTING THE BEST OKRA: When choosing okra at the store, gently press the pointed tip at the end of the pod. Fresh okra should be firm and have a slight snap when pressed. Avoid okra that feels soft or mushy. Additionally, lighter okra pods tend to be more tender and better suited for frying.*

Get ready to discover your new favorite snack! These golden brown okra fries offer a fun and scrumptious alternative to traditional french fries. These irresistibly crisp treats are a lighter choice, perfect for dipping.

Prepare the Okra: Wash the okra thoroughly and pat them dry with a clean kitchen towel. Washing them a few hours before cooking allows extra time for drying.

Cut the Okra: Trim off the hard tops of the okra pods. Then, cut each okra lengthwise into four to six pieces, depending on their size. Aim for even-sized pieces for even cooking.

Make the Coating: In a bowl, whisk together the gram flour, dried mango powder, red chili powder, cumin powder, and sea salt.

Marinate the Okra: Add the sliced okra to the seasoned flour mixture and toss gently to coat them evenly. Let the okra marinate in the coating for 15–20 minutes. This allows the flour to adhere better and prevents excessive flaking during frying.

Fry the Okra: Heat oil in a large pan over medium–high heat. To test if the oil is hot enough, carefully drop a small piece of the okra coating into the oil. If it sizzles immediately, the oil is ready. Gently add a few okra slices to the hot oil in batches, being careful not to overcrowd the pan, as this will lower the oil temperature. Fry for about 2 minutes per side or until the okra is golden brown and crispy. Remove the fried okra with a slotted spoon and drain on a plate lined with paper towels.

Adjust Heat if Needed: If the okra browns too quickly, reduce the heat to medium–low. Fried okra has a wonderful tendency to stay crispy much longer than other fried vegetables, so you don't need to worry about it becoming soggy.

Serve and Enjoy: Finish the crispy okra fries with a generous sprinkle of chaat masala for a bright and tangy flavor. Serve with tamarind sauce for dipping.

Samosas: Around the World in a Pocket

Samosas hold a special place in my heart. These crispy, golden parcels, filled with savory goodness, are a celebration of the fascinating interplay of international cuisines. There's debate about their origin, with some tracing them back to ancient Egypt, others to Persia. But one thing is certain—the concept of fried, savory pastries filled with delicious fillings has captivated palates across continents for centuries. Think of the Cornish pasty of England, the Empanada of Latin America, or the Jamaican patty—all distant cousins of the samosa, united by their reliance on fried dough and flavorful fillings.

The samosa's journey around the world is evident in the delightful array of fillings it has embraced. In Central Asia, "samsa" offer a baked alternative, often filled with spiced ground lamb or sweet pumpkin. East Africa boasts "sambusa" brimming with savory beef or hearty lentils, while Indonesian "samosas" surprise with unique additions like noodles or even sweet concoctions. These global flavors, woven together by the common thread of fried dough, are a beautiful evidence to food's power to connect us across borders and cultures.

Remembering the Magic of Street Food, Made Fresh

Growing up in Nepal, samosas were a quintessential street food. I can still picture the vendors with their giant cauldrons of oil, frying up batches of fifty at a time. The aroma of spices mingled with the anticipation of that first crispy bite filled with potato, pea and masala—was pure childhood bliss! Each samosa cost a mere Rs 5 (5 cents) back then, and the line would snake around the corner, everyone eager for a taste of piping hot goodness dipped in tangy tamarind and tomato chutneys.

Sadly, times have changed. The focus on mass production has often come at the expense of quality. Frozen, premade samosas have become the norm, leaving the true flavor and experience behind. This is what fueled my passion for making samosas at home. Yes, it takes a bit more time and effort. But the reward is immense. Homemade samosas allow me to explore endless possibilities. This recipe features my favorite black chickpea (chana) filling, but the beauty lies in the versatility. From semolina flour to mixed vegetables, carrot, and beans, the fillings are limited only by your imagination!

This isn't just about recreating a childhood memory; it's about celebrating the global love for creative, flavorful fried pastries. So, skip the frozen aisle, grab your favorite fillings, and set out on your own samosa journey. With each delicious bite, you'll be connecting to a rich culinary heritage that spans continents and centuries.

Samosa / Fried Potato Pastry

WRAPPED IN TRADITION: A HANDFUL OF HAPPINESS

For a perfect complement to your crispy samosas, pair them with a refreshing dip like a tamarind sauce, mint chutney, or a cool and creamy sunshine yogurt dip to balance the rich flavors.

INGREDIENTS

Filling

1 cup black chickpeas (chana), dried
4 cups water for soaking
35 oz (990 g) Yukon potatoes
3 tablespoons olive oil
½ tablespoon cumin seeds
1 tablespoon ginger, finely chopped
4 green chilies, chopped
1 cup red onion, finely chopped
½ tablespoon cumin powder
½ teaspoon turmeric
1 teaspoon garam masala
2½ teaspoons dried mango powder
1½ teaspoons salt
½ cup cilantro, chopped
¼ cup green onions, chopped
5 cups oil for frying

Dough

4 cups (600 g) all-purpose flour
1½ teaspoons carom seed
1½ teaspoons salt
150 mL (12 tablespoons) olive oil
200 mL (14 tablespoons) water

TIPS

- *ACHIEVING CRISPY SAMOSAS: The key to crispy samosas is taking the time to thoroughly rub the oil into the flour mixture. This creates a flaky crust. Also, fry them over medium–low heat (level 3 on an electric stove) to ensure they cook evenly and avoid bubbling.*
- *OIL/FLOUR RATIO: I like to use one-fourth part oil to flour.*
- *BAKING OPTION: Bake samosas at 400°F on the middle rack until they are golden brown and crispy, about 30 minutes.*

Crispy, flaky pastry envelopes a flavorful filling of spiced potatoes and chickpeas in these classic Indian samosas. Golden pocket of pure flavor.

Cook the Chickpeas: Rinse and soak the dried chickpeas in 4 cups of water overnight. The next day, pour the chickpeas, water, and a pinch of salt into a saucepan. Cook on medium–high heat. Bring to a boil, then reduce heat to medium–low. Simmer for 30 minutes or until the chickpeas are tender. Alternatively I like to cook chickpeas in an Instant Pot in high pressure settings for 10 minutes. Let pressure release naturally for 20 minutes, then manually release any that remains.

Drain the Chickpeas: Drain the cooked chickpeas and transfer them to a large mixing bowl to cool. You can reserve cooked chickpea water for use in soups or curries.

Boil the Potatoes: While the chickpeas are cooking, wash the potatoes. Place them in a separate pot and cover completely with water. Bring to a boil over medium–high heat, then reduce heat to medium. Simmer for about 30 minutes or until the potatoes are tender. You can check if they're done by poking them with a knife—it should go through easily. Drain the cooked potatoes and set them aside to cool. You can cut the potatoes in half to speed the cooling process.

Make the Dough: Follow the dough steps on the next page.

Make the Filling: While the dough rests, prepare the samosa filling. Peel the boiled potatoes and lightly crush them with your fingers or a fork. Heat 3 tablespoons of oil in a pan over medium heat. Add cumin seeds and let them sizzle for a few seconds. Add ginger and green chilies and sauté for a few seconds until fragrant. Add chopped onion and cook until golden brown. Turn the heat to low and stir in cumin powder, turmeric, and garam masala. Mix well to combine all the spices. Add the crushed potatoes, chickpeas, salt and dried mango powder. Combine everything thoroughly. Taste and adjust the salt as needed. Add 6–8 tablespoons of water, mix and cook for another minute to allow the flavors to meld. Stir in the chopped cilantro and green onions. Remove from the heat and let the filling cool completely before using. I always make more filling than I need. That way, I can save it for later and easily make wraps or enjoy it with rice.

Wrap the Samosas: Follow the wrapping steps on the next page.

How to Wrap Samosa

1. Mix Flour: Sift flour into a large bowl. Add salt and carom seeds. Combine everything and create a well in the center. Gradually pour oil into the well and use your fingers to rub the mixture about 10 minutes until the mixture resembles coarse breadcrumbs.

2. Knead Dough: As you knead, incorporate water gradually, a few tablespoons at a time. Continue until a dough ball forms. The dough should be firm and pliable, not soft. Cover with a damp cloth and let it rest for 2 hours. This allows the gluten to relax, making the dough easier to roll out later.

3. Roll the dough: Knead the dough for a few minutes. Divide the dough into nine equal pieces, approximately 100 grams each. Roll each piece into an oval shape about 5 inches in diameter and 7 inches long. Cover unused portions with a damp towel to prevent from drying.

4. Brush Dough: Cut the dough in half. Roll each half several more times until it reaches a thickness of about 1 millimeter for a crispy texture. Prepare a small bowl of water. Dip a brush into the water and apply it to all sides of the dough. If you don't have a brush, use your fingertips.

5. Make A Cone: Bring the two ends of the dough together and overlap them by half an inch to form a cone shape. Pinch the edges together from the top to the bottom point to seal the cone completely.

6. Add Filling: Fill with about 3 tablespoons of samosa filling, leaving enough space at the top to seal the samosa.

7. Close Samosa: Fold the back of the cone to create a pleat, then pinch it closed to the front of the cone. Seal the samosa by firmly pinching the edges together. Place the finished samosa on a plate covered with a clean tea towel to prevent it from drying out. Repeat the process. Begin frying when you have at least four samosas ready.

8. Fry Samosa: Heat oil in a deep pan over medium–low heat (250°F to 300°F) and carefully add 4 samosas into the hot oil. Fry for 15 minutes or until they are firm and light golden brown. Then increase heat to medium and fry for another 8–10 minutes, until golden brown. Use a slotted strainer to take the samosa out on a plate. Return heat to medium–low to let the oil cool slightly before frying the next batch. Repeat with the remaining samosas. Serve hot with tamarind sauce. Enjoy!

Samosa Chaat

LIGHT & LIVELY: A BURST OF SAVORY SPICES

Enjoy this delicious samosa chaat with a cup of your favorite tea on the side. Elevate your meal by making dumplings to complement the main dish.

INGREDIENTS

6 samosas (page 134)

Yogurt Sauce
1 cup vegan yogurt
1 teaspoon red onion, finely chopped
1 green chili, finely chopped
1 small cucumber, finely chopped
Pinch of salt
Pinch of black pepper

Garnish
½ cup pomegranates
2 tablespoons cilantro, finely chopped
2 tablespoons red onion, finely chopped
1 teaspoon chaat masala

Sauce
Tamarind Sauce (page 34)
Mint Chutney (page 40)

TIPS

- *MAKE IT YOUR OWN: Play with the toppings and sauces to find your perfect flavor combo.*
- *SHORTCUT ALERT: Store-bought samosas work great!*
- *EXTRA CRUNCH? Add peanuts or bhujia (fried chickpea noodles) for some texture fun.*
- *FEELING FRUITY? Try adding thinly sliced apple or banana for a surprising twist!*

You haven't truly experienced Indian street food until you've tried samosa chaat! The name "chaat" means "to lick" in Hindi, and trust me, you'll want to lick your plate clean. Crispy samosa pieces are topped with creamy yogurt sauce, tangy chutneys, and many other delicious toppings.

Prepare the yogurt sauce: In a bowl, combine all the ingredients for the yogurt sauce and gently fold them together until well mixed.

Assemble the Chaat: On a large platter or plate, spread a few tablespoons of yogurt sauce to create a base. Break warm and crispy samosas into bite-sized pieces and arrange them on top of the yogurt sauce. Add a few more tablespoons of yogurt and sprinkle onion over the samosa pieces.

Add the Sauces: Drizzle your desired amount of tamarind sauce and mint chutney over the samosas.

Top it Off: For a burst of sweetness and crunch, sprinkle some pomegranate seeds on top. Add a touch of chaat masala for a delightful blend of sweet, savory, and tangy flavors.

Garnish and Enjoy: Finish your samosa chaat with freshly chopped cilantro and serve immediately. Enjoy!

Across Time and Tastes

As I curled up on the couch, a wave of nostalgia washed over me. My mind wandered through a tapestry of recipes, each one a thread woven from encounters with amazing chefs from around the globe. I remembered the irresistible chicken kofta balls I used to make, bursting with flavor. But over a decade ago, as I embraced a more plant-based lifestyle, meat slowly faded from my cooking repertoire.

This memory sparked a new idea: could I create a satisfying plant-based alternative to those beloved kofta balls? My vision was a flavorful "meatball" made from vegetables, bathed in a fragrant tomato sauce redolent with warm spices.

My experimentation began. Various beans were auditioned for the starring role, each offering a unique texture. But black chickpea, with its slightly firmer bite, stood out, delivering a satisfyingly "meaty" experience. These delightful falafelballs quickly became a mainstay in my kitchen.

From Hoagie to Fettuccine: A Delicious Evolution

Initially, the falafelballs were destined for a hoagie—a sandwich I'd never experienced even during my meat-eating days. The irony wasn't lost on me! To my surprise, the creation was a resounding success. My husband declared it the best hoagie he'd ever tasted, vegan or otherwise.

But the story doesn't end there. One day, with leftover falafel balls on hand, inspiration struck again. I started by boiling some fettuccine. The long, elegant noodles were a perfect canvas for the satisfying spheres. This "falafelball fettuccine" turned out to be a revelation! Honestly, I couldn't decide which version—hoagie or pasta—I enjoyed more. Whenever I make falafelballs, I double the batch to ensure a delightful lunch of hoagies and a hearty dinner of falafel fettuccine.

This recipe isn't just about a tasty vegetarian meal, it's about exploring the amazing ways different cuisines come together and how creative we can be in the kitchen. The playful spirit of falafel extends far beyond hoagies and fettuccine. Imagine these versatile bites nestled in fluffy pita bread, drizzled with tahini sauce and vibrant chopped vegetables, transforming into a delightful vegan gyro. Or try them alongside grilled bell peppers and onions, their smoky char complementing fluffy rice in a comforting Buddha bowl. The possibilities are truly endless! This recipe is your gastronomic passport to exciting new plant-based destinations, with the falafel as your delicious guide.

Falafelball Fettuccine

THE PERFECT BLEND OF TEXTURES: A MATCH MADE IN HEAVEN

This Falafelball fettuccine is a burst of Mediterranean flavors in a classic Italian dish. If you're feeling adventurous, enjoy it with grilled or baked vegetables.

INGREDIENTS

2 cups dry black chickpeas (chana)
4 cups water for soaking
1 tablespoon garlic, minced
1 tablespoon ginger, minced
2 small habaneros, finely chopped
1 teaspoon whole allspice pepper
1 teaspoon nutmeg powder
2-inch long cinnamon stick
6 pods cardamom
1 teaspoon cumin seeds
1 teaspoon coriander seeds
10 cloves
1 anise
¼ cup olive oil
1 bunch cilantro, finely chopped
2 teaspoons sea salt
17 oz (480 g) extra firm tofu, crumbled
1½ cups red onions, finely chopped
¼ cup chickpea flour (besan)
3 tablespoons toasted sesame seeds
6 oz (170 g) fettuccine

Sauce
2 cups Marinara (page 26)

TIPS

- *LEFTOVERS MADE EASY: This recipe yields about seventy-five falafel balls. Store leftover baked falafel balls in an airtight container in the refrigerator for up to a week. Enjoy them in sandwiches, salads, or as a tasty snack.*
- *STAY SAUCY: Feel free to switch up the sauce to diversify your pallet. This is amazing with any Alfredo or my Cilantro Pesto from page 24.*

Cook the Chickpeas: Wash and soak the chickpeas in 4 cups of water overnight. Cook them with 1 teaspoon of salt in an Instant Pot for 6 minutes on high pressure. Alternatively, boil them in a pot until tender (about 30 minutes). Drain the cooked chickpeas, reserving ½ cup of the cooking water.

Make the Falafel Base: In a food processor, pulse the cooked chickpeas with ½ cup of reserved cooking water for about 20 seconds, until they are coarsely ground. You want a chunky texture, not a completely smooth paste. If the mixture is too dry add more water, a tablespoon at a time. Transfer the coarsely ground chickpeas to a large bowl.

Prepare the Spices: Heat a pan over medium heat. Add allspice pepper, cinnamon stick, cardamom, anise, cumin seeds, coriander seeds, and cloves. Dry-roast the spices for a few minutes until fragrant, stirring frequently. Let them cool slightly. In a mortar and pestle or spice blender, blend the spices.

Combine the Falafel Mixture: Add the ground spices, nutmeg powder, crumbled tofu, gram flour, onion, remaining salt, habanero, oil, sesame seeds, and chopped cilantro to the bowl with the chickpea mixture. Gently combine, keeping the tofu in small chunks. Cover the bowl and refrigerate the falafel mixture for at least an hour (or up to two hours for best flavor).

Bake the Falafel Balls: Preheat oven to 400°F (200°C). Line a baking sheet with parchment paper. Take about 1 tablespoon of the falafel mixture and roll it into a ball between your palms to form smooth, round balls. Arrange the balls in rows on the prepared baking sheet. Bake the falafel balls for 40 minutes, flipping them over halfway through baking. Take the falafel balls out and let them cool.

Cook the Fettuccine: Bring a pot of water to a boil. Add a pinch of salt and cook the fettucine according to package instructions for al dente texture (usually around 10 minutes). Drain the pasta and toss it with a drizzle of olive oil.

Assemble and Enjoy: Gently warm the marinara sauce in a saucepan over low heat. Add the falafel balls and simmer for 10 minutes to infuse the flavors. Arrange the cooked fettuccine to a serving plate. Top with the baked falafel balls and marinara sauce. Garnish with cilantro and enjoy!

Holy Basil Udon

SUMMERTIME EUPHORIA: NOODLE NIRVANA

Fragrant basil, chewy udon noodles, and cilantro pesto create a vibrant base. While the crisp carrots and earthy spinach and beets add layers of texture and depth. It's a dish you won't soon forget.

INGREDIENTS

1 cup fresh holy basil leaves
195 mL (14 tablespoons) water
2 cups (300 g) all-purpose flour
½ cup (65 g) corn flour
1½ teaspoons salt
½ cup corn flour for dusting
2 cups baby spinach
2 small carrots, thinly sliced
1 medium orange beet

Sauce
2 tablespoons Cilantro Pesto (page 24)

TIPS

- *NO PASTA MAKER? NO PROBLEM! While a pasta machine makes rolling easier, you can achieve similar results with the Ziploc bag kneading method.*
- *REST THE NOODLES: Let the noodles rest in a warm spot for about an hour in the summer, or 2-3 hours in the winter, so the gluten can relax.*
- *CUSTOMIZE YOUR NOODLES: Feel free to adjust the thickness of the noodles to your preference.*
- *LEFTOVERS MADE EASY: Store leftover cooked noodles in an airtight container in the refrigerator for up to three days. To maximize your time, I usually double the recipe and freeze half of the cooked noodles for later use.*

Blend the Holy Basil: Wash the holy basil leaves. Blend it with water in a blender until smooth.

Make the Dough: In a bowl, combine all-purpose flour, corn flour, and salt. Create a well in the center and gradually add the basil water, mixing with your fingers until a crumbly dough forms. Knead for 10 minutes until the dough comes together into a ball. Cover with a damp cloth and let it rest at room temperature for 2–3 hours to allow the gluten to relax, making the dough more pliable and smooth.

Roll the Dough: Cut the dough into three equal pieces. Generously dust each piece with corn flour to prevent sticking during rolling. Using a pasta machine, begin rolling out the dough at the widest setting, passing it through the machine four to five times. Gradually decrease the thickness setting (I use an electric pasta machine and my settings go from 6 to 5 to 4 to 3). Pass the dough through each setting several times until you achieve a thickness of 2–3 mm. Dust the dough with additional corn flour as needed to prevent sticking. Stack the sheets of dough with plenty of corn flour between the layers to prevent them from adhering. Using a sharp knife, cut the dough lengthwise into noodles approximately ½-inch wide.

Alternative Without a Pasta Machine: Place the rested dough in a two-gallon Ziploc bag between two kitchen towels. Knead the dough with your feet by walking back and forth in circles, flattening from the center outward. Remove the dough, fold it into quarters, and return it to the bag. Repeat this process four times. Generously flour a work surface with corn flour. Transfer the flattened dough to the floured surface. Using a rolling pin, press down on the center of the dough and roll downward, then upward, applying even pressure. Roll the dough out to a thickness of 2–3 mm, rotating it 90 degrees after each pass. Sprinkle with corn flour, fold the dough into thirds, and then cut it into noodles, ranging from ¼ to ½-inch in width. Separate the noodles by lightly dusting them with additional corn flour.

Cook the Noodles: Bring a large pot of water to a boil, then reduce the heat to medium. Gently shake excess flour from noodles and add to the water. Stir with chopsticks to prevent sticking. Cook for 3 minutes, or until the noodles are al dente. Drain and rinse the noodles with cold water for few seconds. Heat a pan, add cilantro pesto. Sauté thinly sliced carrots and beets for 3 minutes, until slightly tender. Add cooked udon and spinach, mix well. Add salt if needed. Remove from heat. Serve and enjoy!

Spicy Tofu Seaweed Wrap

TASTE OF THE SEA: A WORLD TOUR IN A WRAP

The wrap is delicious on its own, but the addition of a light strawberry and walnut salad creates a perfect balance of flavors and textures.

INGREDIENTS

1½ cups sushi rice (medium short grain)
2 cups water
1 tablespoon sake (cooking rice wine)
1 (2x2-inch) small kombu sheet
120 mL (½ cup) rice vinegar
1½ teaspoons salt
1 medium-size cucumber, thinly sliced
1 avocado, pitted and sliced
½ bell pepper, thinly sliced
2 teaspoons toasted sesame seeds
6 nori sheets

Marinate tofu
9 oz (255 g) tofu
1 tablespoon ginger, crushed
¾ teaspoon salt
½ teaspoon turmeric
½ teaspoon cumin powder
1 teaspoon toasted sesame seeds
4 green chilies
4 tablespoons olive oil

TIPS

- *SPICE IT UP (OR DOWN): Control the heat by adjusting the chili powder in the marinade to suit your preference.*
- *GET CREATIVE: This recipe is a playground for customization! Feel free to experiment with different vegetables and fillings to create your perfect wrap.*
- *NO SUSHI MAT? You can use Saran Wrap as well.*

This recipe is my go-to for a quick, easy, and totally delicious dish—perfect for family gatherings! Spicy tofu, fresh veggies, and creamy avocado all wrapped up in nori and rice, creating an irresistible meal.

Marinate the Tofu: Wash the tofu and pat it dry with a kitchen towel. Cut the tofu into long, thin (½-inch) pieces and place it in a bowl. In a mortar and pestle (or small blender), combine all the spices and grind into a paste. Add the paste to the bowl and marinate the tofu by hand. Cover and let the tofu marinate for 30 minutes in the refrigerator.

Prepare the Rice: Rinse the rice in a big bowl four times until the water becomes clear. Drain the rice thoroughly. Transfer the rice into a saucepan and add 2 cups of water. Cover and let it rest for 30 minutes. Heat the saucepan over medium heat. Add sake and kombu on top. Cover the lid and bring it to a boil. Reduce the heat to low and simmer for another 10 minutes.

Meanwhile, mix rice vinegar and salt in a small bowl until the salt dissolves. Once the rice is cooked, turn off the heat and fluff it with a spatula. Let it cool for 10 minutes. Transfer the rice to a large mixing bowl. Pour the vinegar mixture over the rice and gently combine.

Fry the Tofu: While the rice is cooling, heat a pan on medium and add oil. Fry the tofu, cooking 2–3 minutes each side until golden brown.

Prepare the Wrap: Lay a sheet of nori on a bamboo sushi mat, rough side facing up. Dip your fingers in a bowl of water to prevent them from sticking. Spread about one cup of rice evenly over the nori, leaving about a ½-inch space at the bottom where you start rolling and ¾-inch on top (the far edge). Arrange the fillings parallel to the long edges on the lower half of the nori. Sprinkle with some toasted sesame seeds. Carefully lift the bottom edge of the nori and fold it over the fillings. Gently but firmly squeeze the roll with the bamboo mat to create a compact shape. Hold the filling in place and continue rolling until the nori is sealed. Hold for about 10 seconds at the end.

Cut and Serve: Carefully remove the bamboo mat and place the roll on a cutting board. Cut the roll into two to eight equal pieces using a sharp knife, wiping the blade with a damp cloth between cuts to prevent sticking. Repeat with the remaining nori. Transfer the sliced rolls to a plate, drizzle with spicy peanut sauce, and enjoy!

Japchae / Sweet Potato Noodle

GLASS NOODLE GLORY: VEGAN STIR-FRY AT ITS FINEST

The umami-rich stir-fry, with its glorious crunch and juiciness, is perfectly paired with either a seaweed wrap or juicy dumplings.

INGREDIENTS

6 oz (170 g) sweet potato noodles
5 tablespoons sesame oil
15 oz (425 g) shiitake mushrooms, dried
2 cloves garlic, sliced
2 green chilies, chopped
1½ teaspoons salt
½ cup yellow onion, thinly sliced
1 cup red bell pepper, thinly sliced
1 cup yellow bell pepper, thinly sliced
1 cup red cabbage, shredded
2 small (5 oz) carrots, julienne
2 cups green onion, lightly chopped
¼ teaspoon freshly ground black pepper
2 tablespoons toasted sesame seeds
Spicy tofu (page 146, optional)

TIPS

- *MEAT MAGIC WITH MUSHROOMS: Dried shiitake mushrooms offer a satisfyingly meaty texture, making them a fantastic vegan alternative. They're conveniently available presliced in most grocery stores.*
- *FEEDING A CROWD? NO PROBLEM! This recipe is easily doubled or tripled to accommodate a larger group, making it perfect for potlucks or gatherings.*
- *LEFTOVER LOVE: Store any leftover noodles in an airtight container in the refrigerator for up to 2 days. They'll be perfect for a quick and delicious lunch the next day!*

Inspired by classic Korean Japchae, this vibrant vegan version features the meaty texture of shiitake mushrooms, springy sweet potato noodles, and a colorful mix of crunchy vegetables.

Cook the Noodles: Bring a pot of water to a boil. Add the noodles and cook for 7 minutes. Drain the noodles thoroughly and rinse briefly with cold water to stop the cooking process. Toss with 2 teaspoons of sesame oil to prevent sticking.

For meal prep, consider cooking a full package of noodles and refrigerating half for future use.

Cook the Mushrooms: Rehydrate dried shiitake mushrooms by soaking them in hot water for 10 minutes. Heat 2 tablespoons of sesame oil in a pan over medium heat. Add the garlic and green chilies and sauté for a few seconds until fragrant. Squeeze out the excess water from the soaked mushrooms. Add them to the pan, season with a pinch of salt, and cook for about 5 minutes, until golden brown. Remove from the pan and set aside on a plate.

Sauté the Vegetables: Heat the remaining sesame oil in a wok or large pan over medium heat. Add the onion and sauté for a few seconds until fragrant. Add the bell peppers and cook for about 5 minutes, until they begin to soften and develop a golden-brown color. Add the cabbage, carrot, and green onion. Stir-fry for another minute until just wilted. Season with salt and freshly ground black pepper. Add mushroom and mix well.

Assemble the Japchae: Reduce the heat to low. Add the cooked noodles to the pan and carefully toss them with the vegetables, ensuring they are well combined. Turn off the heat.

Serve and Enjoy: Garnish with toasted sesame seeds and tofu (if using). Enjoy!

Paalak Plantain

ISLAND MEETS INDIA: UNEXPECTED FLAVORS, UNFORGETTABLE TASTE

Embrace the classic comfort of lachha paratha for scooping up your creamy paalak plantain, or opt for fluffy basmati rice.

INGREDIENTS

2 large green plantains, unripe
2 tablespoons olive oil
1 teaspoon cumin seeds
2 dried red chilies
½ cup red onion, diced
2 green chilies, finely chopped
1 teaspoon ginger, minced
1 teaspoon garlic, minced
⅛ teaspoon turmeric
1 teaspoon cumin powder
1 teaspoon coriander powder
2 medium (300 g) tomatoes
1 teaspoon salt
4 cups (500 g) spinach, washed
Fresh cilantro for garnish

TIPS

- *HEAT WATCH: If the plantains brown too quickly, reduce the heat.*
- *CREAMY TWIST: For richer flavor, add a splash of coconut milk with the tomatoes.*
- *PACKED WITH GOODNESS: Plantains are a common food in many cultures and are full of nutrients. They're a delicious way to add variety to your meals!*
- *PLANTAIN INSPIRATION: Plantains, a staple in Indian and African cooking, offer a texture similar to paneer, making them a delicious substitute in this recipe.*

Paalak paneer is a popular Indian dish made with spinach and paneer (cottage cheese). This recipe offers a delicious and nutritious twist on paalak paneer and uses fiber, potassium, carbohydrate, and folate-rich plantains instead of cottage cheese.

Prepare the Plantains: Wash the plantains. Peel the skin with a knife and cut them into bite-sized pieces (about 1 inch thick).

Steam the Plantains: Boil water in a steamer. Steam the plantain pieces in a steamer over boiling water for 10 minutes, or until tender. Transfer the steamed plantain to a plate and let them cool slightly.

Sauté the Aromatics: Heat oil in a pan over medium heat. Add the cumin seeds and dried red chilies. Let them sizzle for a few seconds until fragrant. Add the chopped red onion and sauté for a few minutes, until it begins to soften and turn a light golden brown. Add the green chilies and stir to combine.

Add Spices and Plantains: At low heat, add the ginger and garlic paste. Stir in the cumin powder, turmeric powder, and coriander powder. Cook for about 30 seconds, allowing the spices to release their aroma. Add the plantains and mix well, ensuring they are coated in the spices.

Simmer the Sauce: Add the chopped tomatoes and salt to the pan. Stir well to combine. Cover the pan and increase the heat to medium. Simmer for 5 minutes, or until the tomatoes have softened and a light gravy has formed.

Add Spinach: Add the freshly chopped spinach to the gravy. Combine well and cook for about a minute, or until the spinach wilts. Adjust the water to achieve your desired gravy consistency.

Serve and Enjoy: Garnish with fresh cilantro and enjoy!

Dosa: A Taste of South Indian History

The dosa is a South Indian culinary icon. It boasts a history stretching back centuries, likely originating in Tamil Nadu. The hot and humid climate of the region likely drove its development as a method for preserving rice. The fermentation process not only prolonged its life but also unlocked deeper flavors and made it easier to digest.

From the everyday street corner to the most festive occasion, the dosa is a culinary star. Its simple yet exquisite combination of fermented batter, crisp texture, and a symphony of fillings creates a true masterpiece.

My Voyage to Crispy Perfection

I love South Indian food. The exciting flavors and fragrant spices are just incredible. Growing up, my mom's idli and sambar were a staple in our house. But for some reason, we never had dosas at home. Those crispy crepes always looked so good at street food stalls. However I'm not a fan of greasy food and every dosa I tried outside was just too oily.

This love-hate relationship with dosa fueled my desire to recreate it in my home kitchen. The appeal of a light, crispy crepe filled with a flavorful, nongreasy potato masala filling was irresistible. Making it myself meant I could control the oil, unlike the greasy street food versions. This lead to much healthier and more enjoyable dosa.

After several attempts, I mastered the art of achieving that perfect dosa crisp. It's all about the batter—the right balance of fermentation and consistency is key. Yet the real revelation came when I started experimenting with fillings. Tempeh, a fermented soybean cake, quickly became a favorite. Its subtle, nutty flavor adds a delightful complexity to the classic potato filling.

This recipe is an invitation to join me on a dosa-making quest! I encourage you to get creative with fillings like tofu, walnuts, or even shredded cabbage. Use this recipe as your starting point, and soon you'll be enjoying crispy, flavorful dosas at home, week after week.

Tempeh Masala Dosa

WORSHIP AT THE TANGY TEMPLE: TASTE THE MAGIC

Unwrap the flavors of South India! Enjoy your piping hot tempeh masala dosa with tantalizing mango chutney, marinara, or spicy timur sauce.

INGREDIENTS

Batter

½ cup black gram (urad dal without skin)
¼ teaspoon fenugreek seeds
2 tablespoons chana dal
⅓ cup flattened/beaten rice (poha)
1½ cups basmati rice or sona masoori
4 cups water for soaking
1 teaspoon salt

Fillings

4 oz (110 g) tempeh
17 oz (480 g) potatoes
2 tablespoons coconut oil
½ teaspoon mustard seeds
1 teaspoon cumin seeds
4 sprigs fresh curry leaves
1 cup red onion, finely chopped
2 green chilies, finely chopped
1 tablespoon ginger and garlic paste
1 teaspoon cumin powder
½ teaspoon turmeric
1½ tablespoons lemon juice
1 teaspoon sea salt

TIPS

- *FERMENTATION TRICK: I soak the mix in the morning, grind them in the evening and ferment it overnight. During summer, fermentation is not a problem, but during winter, I like to turn the warm setting in my oven for 5 minutes. Then, turn the oven off and place the covered bowl inside the oven and let it ferment overnight.*
- *THIN IT OUT: If your dosa batter feels too thick, whisk in few tablespoons of water until it reaches a pourable consistency, similar to pancake batter.*
- *ONION TRICK: Take an onion and cut in half. Use a fork to stick in the onion to make a handle. Spread the oil with the cut side of the onion. It also adds flavor.*

Soak the Lentils and Rice: Add chana dal, black gram, flattened rice, and fenugreek in a bowl. Rinse only once. Soak in 2 cups of water for 4–5 hours. In a separate bowl, rinse the rice 2–3 times. Soak in 2 cups of water for 4–5 hours.

Grind the Batter: Drain the soaked ingredients, reserving the water. Blend lentils with ½ cup soaking water until smooth. Place in a bowl. Blend rice for about 20 seconds with another ½ cup soaking water until coarse. Combine both with hand, adding more water if needed, for a pancake batter consistency.

Ferment the Batter: Cover the batter with a plate and place in a warm place (inside the oven) for overnight fermentation (at least 14 hours). The batter is properly fermented when it has doubled in volume and is foamy. It will also have a tangy smell. Add salt. If needed, add a few tablespoons of water to keep a pancake batter consistency. Gently mix with hand.

Prepare the Potatoes: Wash the potatoes. Place them in a large saucepan and cover completely with water. Bring to a boil over medium–high heat, then reduce heat to medium. Simmer for about 30 minutes or until the potatoes are tender. Drain the cooked potatoes and set them aside to cool. Once cooled, peel the potato skin and break them into bite-sized pieces by hand.

Prepare the Tempeh: Boil water in a steamer and place the tempeh inside the steamer. Steam for 10 minutes. Transfer it to a plate to cool. Crumble the tempeh into small chunks.

Cook the Masala Filling: Heat oil in a pan over medium heat. Add the mustard and cumin seeds. Temper for a few seconds. Add curry leaves, onion, and chilies; sauté until translucent. Add the ginger-garlic paste and crumbled tempeh. Combine well and cook for a minute. Stir in the cumin powder, turmeric, potatoes, lemon juice, and salt. Combine well and cook until the potatoes are golden brown.

Cook the Dosa: Heat a flat griddle over medium–low heat. If it sizzles when sprinkled with water, it's ready. Use a halved onion to spread few drops of oil evenly around the griddle. Pour a ladle full of dosa batter onto the center of the hot griddle. Spread the batter evenly in a circular motion, working from the center outward, to create a thin, delicate crepe. Turn the heat to medium–high. Drizzle 1 teaspoon of oil around the edges. Cook about 2 minutes until the base looks golden and slightly crispy. Add 3–4 tablespoons of the fillings to one side of the dosa or in the center. Using a flat spatula, carefully fold the crepe over the filling to create a half-moon shape or roll twice to form a cylinder shape. Transfer the dosa to a plate and serve immediately with your favorite chutney. Enjoy!

Empanadas Reimagined: A Jackfruit Twist

I'm fascinated by the global synchronicity of flavorful fillings wrapped in dough. From Nepal's fried momos to Mexico's empanadas, Tibet's shabhaley to India's samosas, this culinary concept is universally satisfying.

My love for hand-held treats inspired these Jackfruit Empanadas. I craved the juicy satisfaction of a dumpling, but with a crispier exterior that would also make them easier to store. This recipe combines the delightful crispy texture of fried bread like nimki with the savory comfort of a samosa filling.

Empanadas, likely originated in Spain or Portugal, but their journey across continents has resulted in a fascinating flavor mosaic. Jackfruit's neutral flavor and remarkably meaty texture make it a go-to vegan ingredient. Its adaptability shines in fragrant Thai curries and crispy Indonesian fritters, showcasing its undeniable versatility.

Finding fresh jackfruit can be an adventure, especially in Kentucky where I live. I sometimes have to rely on slightly older fruit. Luckily, Indian and Nepali stores often come to the rescue during the summer. Just be sure to choose a jackfruit that isn't overly dry inside, as this will affect the flavor. I prefer young jackfruit because it has the best flavor, and its seeds are tender and crunchy.

Memories of Fresh Jackfruit

Growing up in Nepal, summer meant indulging in fresh jackfruit. Unlike the canned versions readily available in the US, Nepali jackfruit bursts with authentic flavor. Canning wasn't a common practice when I was young, and our meals celebrated seasonal produce at its peak.

I remember early summers filled with the joy of baby jackfruit—tender, juicy, and bursting with umami. The best part? Vegetable vendors would expertly remove the skin and cut it into pieces, saving you the hassle. The whole market smells like jackfruit. These memories inspired my jackfruit curries, vegetarian versions of my mother's meat dishes. I hope you enjoy this unique and flavorful dish!

Jackfruit Empanada

FIESTA EXOTICA: WRAPPED IN GOLDEN GOODNESS

Enjoy empanadas with mouth-tingling spicy timur sauce and tangy mango chutney. For a full-on tropical vibe, add bold pico de gallo and a dollop of rich guacamole.

INGREDIENTS

13 oz (368 g) jackfruit
3 cups olive oil
½ tesapoon fenugreek seeds
1 teaspoon garlic, minced
1 teaspoon ginger, minced
½ cup red onion, finely chopped
Half bell pepper, finely chopped
1 cup cabbage, finely chopped
1 teaspoon cumin powder
¼ teaspoon turmeric
3 green chilies, finely chopped
½ cup cilantro, finely chopped
1 teaspoon salt

Dough
2 cups (300 g) all-purpose flour
¼ tsp nigella seeds
½ teaspoon salt
75 mL (6 tablespoons) olive oil
8 tablespoons water

Prepare Dough: In a large bowl, combine flour, nigella seeds, and salt. Drizzle the oil over the mixture. Using your fingertips, rub the oil into the dry ingredients for approximately 10 minutes, until the mixture resembles coarse breadcrumbs. Gradually add water, 1 tablespoon at a time, kneading continuously until a firm and smooth dough forms. Cover the bowl with a damp cloth and let the dough rest at room temperature for 2–3 hours, allowing it to become soft and pliable.

Prep the Jackfruit: Using a sharp knife, carefully remove the skin. Cut the jackfruit flesh into large chunks. Place the jackfruit chunks in the Instant Pot and cover completely with water. Cook on high pressure for 6 minutes. For stovetop, place the jackfruit chunks in a large pot and cover them completely with water. Bring to a boil, then reduce heat to medium–low and simmer for about 1 hour, or until the jackfruit is tender when pierced with a fork. Drain the water and place the jackfruit on a plate to cool completely. Once the jackfruit has cooled sufficiently, shred it by hand, ensuring the hard central core is removed.

Sauté the Vegetables: Heat 2 tablespoons of oil in a pan over medium heat. Add the fenugreek seeds and temper them until they turn a dark brown, almost black, and release a fragrant aroma. Stir in the ginger and garlic paste, then add the onion, bell pepper, jackfruit, and cabbage. Sauté for a few minutes, until the vegetables begin to soften. Stir in the cumin powder, turmeric, green chilies, cilantro, and salt. Cover the pan and cook over medium-low heat for 5 minutes, or until the vegetables are tender. Remove from the heat and allow the filling to cool completely.

Shape the Dough: Lightly knead the dough, then divide into 14–15 portions (about 30 g each). Cover unused portions with a damp towel. Roll each portion into a 5-inch circle and about 1 mm thick. Add a spoonful of cooled jackfruit filling, leaving a 1-inch edge. Brush edges with water, fold in half, and press to seal. Crimp with a fork.

Fry the Empanadas: Heat oil in a shallow pan over medium–low heat (250°F to 325°F). Carefully place 4–5 empanadas in the hot oil and fry for about 5 minutes. Increase heat to medium, flip, and continue frying for another 5 minutes, or until golden brown and crispy. Remove with a slotted spatula to a paper towel-lined plate. Repeat with remaining empanadas, ensuring oil returns to correct temperature between batches. Enjoy with your favorite sauce.

TIPS

- *JACKFRUIT TIP: For convenience, consider using precut fresh jackfruit or canned young jackfruit. They both offer excellent flavor.*
- *FILLING FIX: If your jackfruit filling seems dry during the simmering process, simply add a splash of water to moisten it. This filling is also wonderfully versatile! Try using it in dumplings, tacos, or sandwiches for a delicious plant-based meal.*
- *CRISPY PERFECTION: Don't crowd the pan. Fry empanadas in batches for even cooking and ultimate crispiness.*
- *BAKE TO PERFECTION: For a healthier option, bake your empanadas at 375°F for around 30 minutes.*

Chayote Dumpling

A MILDLY MYSTERIOUS TREAT: POCKETFUL OF FLAVOR

To create a memorable meal, serve your chayote dumplings with a side of rich marinara sauce and crispy timur fries.

INGREDIENTS

4 medium (720 g) chayote
⅔ cup red onion, finely chopped
1 teaspoon garlic, minced
1 teaspoon ginger, minced
½ cup green onion, finely chopped
½ cup cilantro, finely chopped
1 teaspoon salt
1 green chili, finely chopped
4 tablespoons olive oil
½ teaspoon fenugreek seeds
½ teaspoon turmeric

Dumpling Dough
2 cups (315 g) all purpose flour
156 mL (11 tablespoons) water

Sauce
Marinara (Page 26)
Spicy Timur Sauce (Page 32)

TIPS

- *FILLINGS & WATER: Adjust fillings to taste. To prevent soggy dumplings, squeeze excess water from chayote using a cheesecloth.*
- *ROLLING & COOKING: Dust rolling pin with flour to prevent sticking. Don't overcrowd the pan when cooking.*
- *CHAYOTE: Younger chayote is preferable due to its softer skin and tender seeds, but mature chayote can also be used. To prepare mature chayote, cut around the seed and peel the skin with a knife.*
- *BATCH COOKING: Make twenty dumplings at a time, cook ten, then continue making dumplings while the first batch cooks. This recipe yields forty to fifty dumplings.*

Cook the Chayote: This unique squash has a mild, slightly sweet flavor like a potato but with a softer texture. Wash the chayote, place it in a pan, cover it fully with water, and bring to a boil. Reduce heat and simmer for 25–30 minutes or until a knife slides in easily. Remove the chayote from the pot and let it cool. Cut it in half, scoop out the seed, and peel the skin gently with knife. Use a fork to mash the chayote and place it in a cheesecloth-lined strainer. Gently squeeze out all the excess water and let it drain for 10 minutes.

Make the Dough: In a mixing bowl, add flour and gradually incorporate water. Knead for about 5 minutes until the dough has a smooth, elastic consistency. Cover the dough with a damp cloth or a plate and let it rest for 30 minutes to an hour.

Prepare the Filling: Heat 2 tablespoons of oil in a pan over medium heat. Temper the fenugreek seeds until they turn a dark brown color, being careful not to burn them. Add the chopped onion and ginger-garlic paste. Stir for about a minute, until the onion softens. Add the turmeric powder, mashed chayote, cilantro, green onion, and salt. Mix well, ensuring all ingredients are evenly coated with the spices. Remove from the heat and let the mixture cool completely. Allow it to marinate for at least 20 minutes for the flavors to blend.

Assemble the Dumplings: Lightly knead the rested dough to smooth it out, then divide it into 10–12-gram portions. On a lightly floured surface, roll each portion into a 3.5-inch circle. Place a spoonful of filling in the center of the wrapper. Fold the wrapper in half, sealing one of the bottom corners (left or right, whichever feels comfortable). Hold the wrapper gently in your secondary hand. With your primary hand, begin creating pleats by pinching a small section of the dough along one edge and folding it slightly over itself. Continue this process, overlapping the pleats as you work your way to the opposite corner. Press firmly along the top edge to ensure a good seal. You can pleat either the front or back edge of the dough. For a simpler shape, fold the dough in half over the filling to form a half-moon shape and pinch the edges tightly to seal.

Cook the Dumplings and Enjoy: Heat a tablespoon of oil in a skillet over medium heat. Carefully arrange about 10 dumplings, leaving about an inch between them. Cook for a few minutes until the bottoms are golden brown. Add ½ cup of water to the pan, cover, and steam for 8 minutes over medium–high heat to ensure the filling is cooked through. Transfer the juicy dumplings to a plate. Enjoy!

Timur Fries

HIMALAYAN HEAT: THE SPICY SPUD SENSATION

Enjoy these fiery fries with my special sauce and guacamole. For a complete meal, pair with the salads, savories, and breads in this book.

INGREDIENTS

18 oz (510 g) russet potatoes
2 tablespoons distilled white vinegar
4 cup olive oil for frying

Spice blend
1 teaspoon timur powder
½ teaspoon dried oregano
½ teaspoon dried mango powder
½ teaspoon red chili powder
½ teaspoon black pepper
¼ teaspoon sea salt
¼ teaspoon garlic powder

Cosmic Cream (Secret Sauce for Fries)
½ teaspoon brown mustard seeds
½ cup cashews
4 tablespoon olive oil
½ teaspoon sea salt
1 tablespoon apple cider vinegar
2 tablespoon lemon juice
1 red chili
2–4 tablespoon water

TIPS

- *BAKED FRIES: Preheat oven to 400°F (200°C). Once the potatoes are parboiled, drain them well and let them cool on a baking tray. Line a baking sheet with parchment paper and arrange the potato sticks in a single layer, making sure they are not overcrowded. Toss the potatoes with a teaspoon of the spice blend and 3 tablespoons of oil, ensuring they are evenly coated. Bake for about 20 minutes, until the bottoms are golden brown and crispy. Flip the sticks carefully and bake for another 20 minutes, or until golden brown and crispy.*

Experience the Himalayas with Timur Fries! Crispy potatoes, infused with timur's citrusy zing, offer a taste of Nepalese cuisine.

Prepare the Potatoes: Choose medium-size starchy potatoes. Peel the skin and cut in half. Slice the halves lengthwise into ¼-inch sticks. Soak the potato sticks in a bowl of cold water for 30 minutes. This soaking process helps to remove excess starch.

Parboil the Potatoes: In a large pot, combine the potatoes, white vinegar, and sufficient water to cover. Bring to a simmer over high heat, then reduce heat to low and parboil for 10 minutes. The objective is to partially cook the potatoes, rendering them slightly translucent on the exterior while maintaining a firm interior. Overcooking will lead to a mushy texture. Drain the potatoes thoroughly in a colander and spread them in a single layer on a flat baking sheet lined with a kitchen towel to dry and cool completely.

Fry the Potatoes: Heat oil in a large pan or Dutch oven to 400°F. Fry parboiled potatoes in small batches, maintaining consistent oil temperature. Fry each batch for 1 minute on high heat. Remove with a slotted spoon and transfer to paper towels to drain. Repeat with remaining potatoes and allow to cool completely. Reheat the oil to 400°F and fry the potatoes a second time, in batches, for approximately 3–5 minutes, until golden brown. Note that the oil temperature will rise significantly after each batch; reduce the heat to medium between batches to maintain a consistent frying temperature. Remove the finished potatoes with a slotted spoon and drain on paper towels.

Season and Enjoy: Combine the spice blend in a small bowl. While the fries are still warm, toss them with the spice blend to your preferred level, ensuring even coating.

Secret Sauce: This special sauce is a must-try with fries and I felt compelled to share it. Roast brown mustard seeds in a skillet for 5 minutes and allow to cool. Soak cashews in warm water for 30 minutes. Drain and blend the cashews with olive oil, salt, apple cider vinegar, lemon juice, red chili, mustard, and water as needed to achieve the desired consistency. Chill for 30 minutes. This tangy, creamy sauce is perfect for fries or sandwiches, offering a delightful twist on tartar sauce.

Ancient Origins, Modern Delight: The Taco

The famous taco traces its roots to ancient Mesopotamia, where early flatbreads were filled with savory ingredients. This concept spread across continents, evolving into pita bread in the Middle East, roti/chapati in India, and eventually the corn tortilla in Mexico. Today, the taco is an international fundamental, representing a rich culinary history shared by cultures worldwide. From samosas to spring rolls, the filled pocket is a timeless delight.

From Roti to Taco: A Fusion Adventure

Food, like cultures around the world, shares a beautiful commonality—a love for feeding ourselves and our loved ones. We celebrate life's moments with feasts, raise our children with nourishing meals, and find comfort in familiar flavors. The simple taco, a quintessential Mexican dish, is a prime example. But this comfort food has global cousins! In Nepal, we have our "Roti rolls," and India boasts the "Katti roll," both street food staples that share the spirit of the taco—a handheld, delicious combination of fillings wrapped in a soft, flavorful exterior.

Fried vegetables are another thread that weaves cultures together. Zucchini, with its prolific growth habit, is a gardener's delight. Every summer, my zucchini plants explode with life, inspiring endless recipe creations. From hearty curries and savory fried rice to comforting breads and refreshing soups, zucchini finds its way into countless dishes. It even adds a delightful touch to pastas and pizzas!

Here I've used wheat flour for the flatbread, but feel free to embrace your inner explorer and try a corn flour version too! Both options are delicious, and the beauty of this recipe lies in its adaptability.

Tempura's Delicate Dance

Tempura, the airy and light Japanese frying technique featured in this recipe, boasts a fascinating history as well. While deep-frying existed in Japan for centuries, tempura's unique batter and focus on delicate flavors arrived with Portuguese missionaries in the sixteenth century. These early versions used simple ingredients like flour and water, creating a batter that cooked quickly without overwhelming the fillings. Its focus on highlighting fresh, seasonal ingredients through a delicate, crispy coating has made it a beloved technique worldwide. And in Nepal, we have our own delicious version called pakaura/pakora, made with a chickpea flour batter.

Zucchini Tempura Taco

TOKYO MEETS TIJUANA: A SYMPHONY OF BATTERED BRILLIANCE

Crispy vegetable tempura tacos, dressed to impress with marinara, peanut sauce, or chimichurri sauce, plus a tangy margarita. A flavor adventure awaits.

INGREDIENTS

18 oz (510 g) zucchini
A few oyster mushrooms
1 bell pepper, ¼-inch thinly sliced
½ onion, ¼-inch thinly sliced
1 tomato, diced
1 medium cucumber, diced
2 green chilies, finely chopped
¼ cup cilantro, finely chopped
¼ cup green onion, finely chopped
½ teaspoon salt
⅛ teaspoon black pepper
1 tablespoon fresh lime juice
1 avocado, diced
2 cups olive oil
6 tortilla (flatbread/roti)

Tempura Batter
½ cup all-purpose flour
½ cup ice cold water
A pinch of sea salt

TIPS

- *TORTILLA VARIATION: For a truly memorable meal, wrap your tempura tacos in warm, chewy roti or flaky lachha paratha. For a simpler approach, follow aaloo paratha recipe, rolling the dough to 8–9-inches round and cooking on a griddle, omitting the potato filling. Use store-bought tortillas for quicker alternative.*
- *FRY WISELY: To ensure even cooking and maximum crispness, avoid overcrowding the pan. Fry only 3–4 vegetables at a time.*
- *SPICE IT UP: Adjust the green chili in the salad to your desired heat level.*
- *VEGGIE VARIETY: Explore other tempura possibilities. Broccoli florets, carrots, shiitake mushroom, pumpkin, jalapeno, or eggplant work well.*

Experience a flavor burst like no other. A humble taco, transformed by tempura's touch, becomes a delightful combination of crispy vegetables, fresh salad, and creamy avocado.

Prep the Zucchini: Wash and pat dry the zucchini with a kitchen towel. Slice into ¼-inch thick, 2–3-inch long strips. For even cooking, try to make the strips as uniform in size as possible.

Marinate the Vegetables: Tear the mushrooms by hand into bite-sized pieces. In a bowl, combine the sliced zucchini, chopped bell peppers, sliced onion, and the prepared mushrooms. Season the vegetables with salt. Toss well to ensure all the vegetables are evenly coated and set aside to marinate for 10 minutes.

Prepare the Salad: In a separate bowl, combine tomatoes, cucumber, green chilies, cilantro, freshly ground black pepper, a pinch of salt, and lime juice. Cut or scoop avocado into bite-sized pieces and add just before serving to prevent browning.

Prepare the Tempura Batter: Sift the flour into a mixing bowl to remove any lumps. Gradually whisk in ice-cold water, a small amount at a time, until a thin, smooth, and barely combined batter forms. The consistency should be light and fluid, with a visual resemblance to thin, velvety cream rather than the thickness of pancake batter. Use chopsticks to gently incorporate the water for just a few seconds, ensuring optimal texture. Over mixing activates gluten, resulting in a dense and chewy coating. Add a few extra teaspoons of water, if necessary, to fine-tune the consistency.

Fry the Tempura: Heat about 2 inches of oil in a shallow pan over medium–high heat until it reaches 350°F (175°C). Dip each marinated vegetable individually in the tempura batter, ensuring it is completely coated. Carefully lower the battered vegetables into the hot oil, few piece at a time, to avoid overcrowding. Fry for 2–4 minutes, or until they are golden brown and crispy. Use a slotted spatula to remove the tempura from the oil and transfer it to a plate.

Assemble and Enjoy: Warm the tortillas gently. Generously fill each tortilla with the salad mixture, then top with the crispy tempura and chunks of creamy avocado. Drizzle your favorite sauce and squeeze fresh lime juice over the top. Serve the tacos immediately for the best texture and taste.

Bitter Gourd Pickle Salad

THE BEAUTY OF BITTER: A HEALTHY DOSE OF RICHNESS

Spice things up! Serve your Bitter Gourd Salad with crispy tempura or fragrant samosas for a taste sensation you won't forget.

INGREDIENTS

18 oz (510 g) bitter gourd
12 oz (340 g) Yukon potatoes
2 tablespoons olive oil
1 teaspoon salt
1 teaspoon hog plum powder
4 tablespoons water for soaking hog plum
½ red onion, thinly sliced
3 tablespoons sesame powder
1 or 2 tablespoons lemon juice
½ teaspoon turmeric
2 cloves garlic, finely chopped
2 green chilies, finely chopped
Handful of chopped cilantro for garnish

Temper Pickle

2 tablespoon olive oil
½ teaspoon fenugreek seeds

TIPS

- *BITTERGOURD SELECTION: Choose small, young bitter gourds for the most delicate flavor.*
- *ADJUST THE BITTERNESS: For those who prefer milder bitterness, you can skip steaming and boil the bitter gourd until tender. Steaming helps retain some bitterness, which I personally enjoy.*
- *FRY-FREE OPTION: This pickle can also be made without frying. Steam until they are tender. Skip the frying step and proceed directly to the tempering process.*

Discover bitter gourd in this refreshing pickle salad. Its unique flavor, often overlooked, becomes a surprising culinary gem when pickled.

Prep the Bitter Gourd: Wash the bitter gourd thoroughly, trim the ends, and cut it in half lengthwise. Using a spoon, scoop out the seeds. Slice the bitter gourd halves into 2-inch long pieces that are ¼-inch wide.

Steam the Vegetables: Wash the potato thoroughly and cut it in half. In a steamer, combine the sliced bitter gourd and the potato halves. Steam the vegetables over medium heat for 25–30 minutes, or until both the bitter gourd and the potato are tender when pierced with a fork. Transfer the steamed vegetables to a plate and let them cool completely.

Fry the Bitter Gourd: Heat oil in a pan over high heat. Once hot, add the sliced bitter gourd and ½ teaspoon of salt. Fry for 10 minutes, stirring occasionally, until the bitter gourd begins to brown. Transfer the fried bitter gourd to a wide bowl and let it cool completely.

Soak Hog Plum: Soak hog plum in a bowl for 15 minutes. The intense sourness of hog plums creates a sharp and tangy flavor to the pickle.

Combine the Pickle Mixture: While the bitter gourd cools, chop the cooked potatoes into bite-sized pieces. In a large bowl, combine the cooled bitter gourd, sliced onion, lemon juice, freshly ground sesame powder, the remaining salt, and the soaked hog plum. Mix thoroughly with your hands, ensuring all ingredients are well combined.

Add the Finishing Touches: Sprinkle the turmeric powder, chopped green chili, and garlic evenly over the surface of the prepared pickle mixture. Do not mix these ingredients into the salad at this stage.

Temper the Pickle: Heat oil in a small pan over medium heat. Add fenugreek seeds and cook until they crackle and turn a very dark brown, almost black, but not quite. Carefully pour the hot, fragrant oil over the pickle to infuse it with an aromatic flavor. Add chopped cilantro and gently mix the pickle with your hands. Adjust salt and lemon juice to taste. If the mixture is dry, add a little water to loosen it. Garnish with fresh cilantro. Refrigerate for 30 minutes to allow the flavors to blend.

Serve and Enjoy!

Acknowledgments

Life is a magical journey, especially when embracing what nourishes us. To my extraordinary husband Charles, this book is a love letter. Thank you for creating our beautiful life together. Your unwavering support for my passions in gardening, recipe creation, and cookbook design has been instrumental. You've redefined love daily, and your contributions to this second cookbook, from childcare to editing, are invaluable.

A special thank-you to my dear mother-in-law and father-in-law for their constant encouragement and support. To my sister and sister-in-law, thank you for always enjoying my cooking, your belief in me and your inspiration.

To my incredible friends from around the globe, your support has been a constant source of inspiration. This cookbook, *Garden Exotica,* represents a dream come true, from my days as an international student to this moment as an author of international plant-based recipes. I hope it brings you joy and inspires you to create delicious meals in your own kitchens.

Immense gratitude to my wonderful publisher David Husley, lead project manager David Miller, and graphic designer Jennifer Wilder for all your input in creation of this cookbook. Your faith in me and the opportunity to write *Garden Exotica* were a true blessing, especially during a year filled with both immense joy and challenges. Moving back to the US after living in Nepal for three and a half years, welcoming our beautiful daughter Saraswati and starting a home garden—it was a whirlwind! But through it all, the act of creating this book provided a sense of calm and purpose. As I finish writing, Saraswati is now a curious two-year-old who delights in the fresh, organic produce from our garden and the recipes in this cookbook.

This book is a celebration of growth, new beginnings, and the nourishing power of food that comes from the earth and the people we love. Here's to a life filled with delicious creations and unforgettable flavors!

About the Author

Babita Shrestha, the creative mind behind Vegan Nepal, is a plant-based chef, photographer, and graphic designer and the author of the acclaimed *Plant-Based Himalaya*.

Her love affair with food began in Nepal's Terai region, where she learned traditional cooking from her mother, a skill that blossomed into a lifelong passion. Her world expanded further with moves to Kathmandu and then the United States, where she honed her artistic talents, graduating with a Bachelor of Fine Arts degree from St. Cloud State University.

Garden Exotica is a tribute to Babita's multifaceted approach to food. Drawing inspiration from her Nepali roots and global experiences, she creates innovative plant-based dishes that bridge cultures and tantalize the senses. Every element of her cookbooks, from the stunning visuals (a result of her photography and design skills) to the mouthwatering recipes, reflects her dedication and creativity.

Beyond her culinary talents, Babita is a passionate advocate for sustainability. Her cooking philosophy is deeply rooted in her devotion to Ayurvedic practices, the local food movement, organic farming, and her belief in ancestral wisdom. She encourages readers to embrace a healthy and environmentally conscious lifestyle.

Driven by a love of exploration and a desire to reconnect with her roots, Babita returned to Nepal in 2020. Near the majestic Annapurna Mountains, she found inspiration in the fresh produce grown in her backyard and the vibrant culture that surrounded her. Motherhood adds another layer of joy to her life, and she cherishes every moment spent nurturing her family and her love for cooking. Babita currently lives in Lexington, Kentucky, with her husband Charles and daughter Saraswati.

To learn more about Babita:
www.vegannepal.net

INDEX

For Indiana University Press

Tony Brewer *Artist and Book Designer*
Anna Francis *Assistant Acquisitions Editor*
Anna Garnai *Production Coordinator*
Samantha Heffner *Marketing Production Manager*
Katie Huggins *Production Manager*
Alyssa Nicole Lucas *Marketing and Publicity Manager*
Annie L. Martin *Editorial Director*
David Miller *Lead Project Manager/Editor*
Dan Pyle *Online Publishing Manager*
Jennifer Wilder *Senior Artist and Book Designer*